Law in Society Series

DEVIANCE, CRIME
AND SOCIO-LEGAL CONTROL

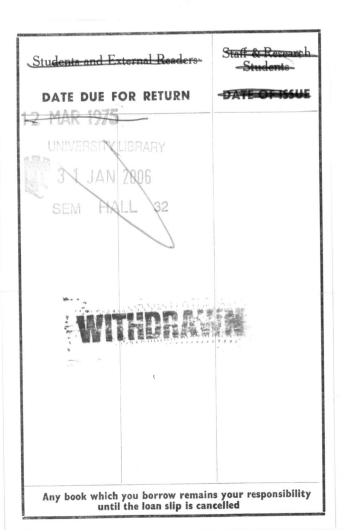

Other publications by the same authors

ROLAND ROBERTSON:
(with J. P. Nettl) *International Systems and the Modernization of Societies* (Faber, 1968)
(edited) *The Sociology of Religion* (Penguin, 1969)
The Sociological Interpretation of Religion (Blackwell, 1970)
Culture and Cultural Change (Blackwell, 1973)

LAURIE TAYLOR:
Deviance and Society (Michael Joseph, 1971)
(with Stanley Cohen) *Psychological Survival* (Penguin, 1972)

Other titles in the series

Social Needs and Legal Action
PAULINE MORRIS, RICHARD WHITE AND PHILIP LEWIS

Knowledge and Opinion About Law
ADAM PODGORECKI, WOLFGANG KAUPEN, J. VAN HOUTTE
P. VINKE, BERL KUTCHINSKY

Deviance, Crime and Socio-Legal Control:
COMPARATIVE PERSPECTIVES

ROLAND ROBERTSON
and LAURIE TAYLOR
UNIVERSITY OF YORK, ENGLAND

Law in Society Series
edited by
C. M. CAMPBELL, W. G. CARSON, P. N. P. WILES

MARTIN ROBERTSON

First published in 1973 by Martin Robertson and Company Ltd, 17 Quick Street, London N1 8HL

ISBN 0 85520 018 9

C

Printed in Great Britain by
The Barleyman Press, Bristol

PREFACE

This monograph is an elaboration of ideas which were initially expressed in a paper given to the Annual Conference of the British Sociological Association in April, 1971, entitled 'Problems in the Comparative Analysis of Deviance: A Survey and a Proposal'. It constitutes the basis for a major research project which the authors are presently undertaking.

We would like to acknowledge the stimulation that we have received from our discussions with graduate students in the Department of Sociology at the University of York. We also wish to thank our colleague, Anne Akeroyd, for a number of very helpful suggestions. Liz Munro and Margaret Silcock have performed secretarial tasks speedily and efficiently.

CONTENTS

INTRODUCTORY NOTE

Lawyers and sociologists in Britain seem to have stood apart from one another. Of course, the study of law was central to the work of some scholars whom we now regard as the architects of modern sociology. But in British sociology this early interest was not maintained or developed, with the result that in the contemporary period we are talking about the idea of a sociology of law as a new growth area. Sociological interest in Britain may have been captured rather late but now, with the encouragement of the Social Science Research Council and research foundations, development is being urgently fostered. This lack of a received tradition of interest in the field of law means that at present there is not the same large number of specialist sociologists such as exists in industrial sociology, sociology of religion, education, or whatever.

The one area where social scientists and lawyers have up to now had fairly extensive contact has been criminology, and it is likely that many of the sociologists who will begin to study law will come from criminology. From the lawyers' point of view this has one major and obvious disadvantage: namely, an exclusive focus on criminal law. In the present monograph Roland Robertson and Laurie Taylor examine how the questions asked by traditional criminology led to what they call an 'imbalance in the social scientist's approach to law and order'. The focus used, they argue, had the undesirable effect of concentrating interest on the etiology of criminal behaviour, to the exclusion of exploring the relationship between behaviour and measures taken to control behaviour. Fortunately, however, over the last decade the traditional boundaries of criminology have been questioned and increasingly broken down. The most obvious outward sign of the change is that many sociologists working in this area would now define their interest as being 'deviance' rather than 'criminology'. As the authors point out this is more than just verbal quibbling since the study of 'deviant behaviour', by which is meant any behaviour which violates the norms of a particular social group and which that group will take steps to control and sanction, moves 'criminology' out of a narrow field defined by the criminal law. This means that sociological attention is now aimed much more broadly at 'deviant behaviour' and 'social control'.

For lawyers the sociologist's use of the word 'deviance' might be off-putting, but they should welcome the move which it signifies because it means that sociologists are increasingly interested in the operation of social norms in general. The narrow boundaries of criminology which made the social scientist's efforts peripheral for so many lawyers have now been abandoned, and the way is open for developing a genuine sociology of law. Initially, to be sure, much of the social scientist's research will still be concentrated on crime. In that area a body of theory and research already exists which it would be folly not to continue to build upon. However, even within studies of crime, the concepts used, and the questions posed, are increasingly such as to allow for the cumulative development of theories about the general relationship between deviance and control.

Robertson and Taylor's paper is an attempt to specify how this new perspective, in what used to be known as 'criminology' can be taken advantage of and developed. The major part of their essay is a cogent argument for the use of comparative analysis in this area. Comparative analysis, by examining the relationship between deviance and social control in different social contexts, allows us to develop generalizations which hold true across time and between cultures. Such a procedure helps to attain that objectivity—through what the authors term 'anthropological distancing'—which will enable us to construct a cumulative body of theory. The methodological prescription of comparative analysis is not, however, an easy one to attain. The recent stress in the social sciences on the notion of relativism in relation to explanation, has acted as a powerful constraint on comparative methodology. Furthermore any comparative analysis must be adequate at the level of meaning: that is, it must ensure that conceptual categories do not just involve word translation but rather translation of situational meaning. In spite of these difficulties the authors believe that the use of the comparative method provides a means for the development of

10

the sociology of law. Their aim is not simply to gain insights into the differences between societies, but to use a comparative method to develop adequate modes of sociological analysis. In other words, they are arguing that theories about social control in general, will enable us to construct theories about law, which will go beyond particularistic descriptions.

The aim of this monograph series is to encourage the development of the sociology of law. As such we hope that the series will be read by both lawyers and sociologists. This, one of the first monographs, illustrates only too clearly the complexity of the task which lies before us. At the present time there seems to be a group of both lawyers and sociologists who are eager to begin the kind of co-operation which will be necessary. It would be a tragedy if this impetus were lost: but the danger exists that our resources may be wasted by concentrating exclusively on answering short-term practical problems. A part of the importance of Robertson and Taylor's paper lies in focusing our attention on the longer term need to develop social scientific explanations. We are very much at the beginning of our study of social control: this paper's contribution is in suggesting a number of directions that our efforts might usefully take.

C.M.C.
W.G.C.
P.N.P.W.

NOTES ON THE AUTHORS

Roland Robertson graduated from Southampton University and has since held teaching positions at the Universities of Leeds, Essex, Pittsburgh, and the Chinese University of Hong Kong. He is now Professor and Head of the Department of Sociology, at the University of York.

His publications include *International Systems and the Modernization of Societies*, Faber, 1968 (with J. P. Nettl); *The Sociology of Religion*, Penguin, 1969 (editor); and *The Sociological Interpretation of Religion*, Blackwell, 1970. Two further books are in preparation: *Culture and Cultural Change*, Blackwell; and *New Directions in the Sociology of Religion*, Blackwell.

His major research interests are the comparative analysis of socio-legal systems, and cultural change in Western societies.

Laurie Taylor is senior Lecturer in Sociology at the University of York. He obtained his first degree at Birkbeck College, University of London, and his higher degree at the University of Leicester. His previous publications include *Deviance and Society* (Michael Joseph 1971), *Psychological Survival: The Experience of Long Term Imprisonment* (written with Stan Cohen. Penguin 1972). His next book *Defiant and the Defeated* (also written with Stan Cohen) will be published later this year by Allen Lane. He is a regular contributor to *New Society* and to *The Times Higher Education Supplement*. His current research is concerned with establishing the phenomenological qualities of differing social situations.

13

(A) APPROACHES TO THE PROBLEM OF DEVIANCE AND CONTROL

(1) *Introduction: Imbalances in Social Scientists' Approaches to Problems of Law and Order*

Of the numerous publicly debated and dramatized social problems of the late 1960's and early 1970's 'law and order' has been one of the most conspicuous. This is not unrelated to the fact that the high visibility of this particular problem has distinct advantages for certain groups in society. Politicians, for example, are often, for good electoral reasons, anxious to cast themselves in the role of combatants in the war against crime, an image whose impact is greatly dependent upon a general public appreciation of the threatening nature of the adversary. Similarly, specialists in mass communication find that increasing the audience for crime 'news' depends upon promoting a generalized belief that law and order is breaking down; it makes good commercial sense that the avid user of the media should come to live in a world which is dominated by crime. This type of exposure to political and mass media stereotypes eventually appears to have real consequences for the public. The American President's Commission on Law Enforcement and Administration of Justice found that crime was perceived by the public as one of the most serious of all domestic problems.[1] Lyndon Johnson may well have been speaking for a large section of the American nation in 1966 when he declared:

> The problems of crime bring us together. Even as we join in common action, we know there can be no instant victory. Ancient evils do not yield to easy conquest. We cannot limit our efforts to enemies we can see. We must with equal resolve, seek out new knowledge, new techniques and new understanding.[2]

15

Professional students have not been slow to respond to the public interest in crime in their writing and research. Indeed in many cases they have become directly involved in the type of war on crime which Johnson described. The President's Crime Commission alone employed hundreds of academic advisers from a variety of disciplines—law, sociology and psychology. The range of issues raised by the law-and-order discussion cut across a large number of areas of specialization, pulling in experts from the sociology of deviance, criminology, the sociology of law, political science and jurisprudence. Unfortunately the high degree of specialization in each of these disciplines, coupled with the discrete manner in which the problem area was defined, inhibited the possibility of such experts coming to terms with significant aspects of the law-and-order theme. As long as the subject remained 'crime', and in particular the etiological approach to crime, then some degree of methodological and conceptual consensus could be maintained. However, once the question of the nature of control—the other dimension of the law-and-order problem—is raised, difficulties begin. The President's Crime Comission avoided dissensus by steering clear of the problem. As Quinney has observed in his discussion of the commission:

No assessment was offered of the use of the criminal law as a sanction for human behaviour. The criminal law as a force in defining and perpetuating crime was not conceived as part of the reality of the crime problem. For the commission, crime is not that which the law defines as criminal, but it is an evil that exists in spite of the law.[3]

The commission was not, however, thoroughly representative of academic opinion. The early expression of the law-and-order theme by conservative American politicians ran against the liberal grain that is such a strong feature of the social scientific community, and Quinney is only one of a number of sociologists who have resisted the stress upon the problem of 'crime', and have instead pointed to the significance of the control aspect in the study of crime and deviance.[4] Regardless of political or philosophical inclination there is now an emergent agreement to the effect that few of the law-and-order problems can be regarded as empirically isolated—that, for example, the comprehension of organized crime

16

cannot be divorced from a variety of social, cultural and psycho-logical, not to say political and economic, factors. This emergent agreement is negatively expressed in the view that law and legal sophistication have serious limitations as independent variables—that is to say, as areas of manipulation which have a strong carry-over in behavioural terms. More positively, but closely connected to the latter view, is the willingness, notably in the public, media-based discussion of crime, to acknowledge and confront the *reality* of the control-deviance relationship, as caught in the utterance 'policemen are only natural; one would expect to find the same amount of crime among policemen as among the population at large'.

This recognition of the complex nature of the inter-relationship between deviants and controllers has become particularly evident in the last ten years in Western industrialized societies, where the incidence of police corruption, and of police infiltration into criminal groups, has become a standard feature of the 'crime scene'. The degree to which there is a need for the police to become law-breakers in order to do their job efficiently has become a matter for public debate.

(2) *The Advantages of a Comparative Perspective*

In this monograph we wish to break into relatively uncharted ground by providing a co-ordinative scheme which will allow for discussion of these and other types of inter-relationships. Our emphasis in this is comparative. We wish to consider the problems of comparing order-deviance phenomena in different kinds of societal context, and to argue for the importance of making generalizations across time and space. A very large proportion of analyses and findings in the area of control and deviance have been developed within and narrowly confined to *particular* social and cultural contexts. Much of the well-known social scientific material applies only to a single context—a town or a community. The attraction of comparative analysis in this type of situation is that it will not merely provide clues to the extrinsic relevance of such single-context studies, but it will also help to make *future* studies less context-specific and provide benchmarks for the assessment

17

of their wider significance. For comparative analysis is basically a universalizing and a cumulative mode of discussion.

A second reason for our attempt to introduce a definite comparative element into the order-deviance problem area is our desire to gain what might be called 'anthropological distance'. We are convinced that the understanding and treatment of seemingly intractable problems is facilitated by 'removing' ourselves from the context of immediate familiarity. Until we can place the taken-for-granted on a par with that which we normally have little to do with, the former will not be seen in any rigorous way. In one sense all analysis of 'local' problems involves distancing. But the more seemingly profound the problem the less easy it is to accomplish such distancing. This is particularly true when we become aware that the way in which we *see* a problem, indeed the very words and concepts which we utilize in the comprehension of it, may be so closely bound up with *the problem itself* that all sense of genuine objectivity is lost from the outset.

It is of course true that the vast majority of social-scientific concepts and thought-patterns are culturally limited, in the sense of having originated within the context of West European and/or North American societies. Recently, however, this limiting circumstance has been debated in several branches of social science. One major form of such concern involves the discussants using primitive societies as supposedly extreme contrast cases and, in effect, attempting to reach a more neutral stance, culturally speaking, via immersion in the distant context. Similar in its effects, if not based on the same ideas, is the increasing tendency for anthropologists to apply their ideas and methods to modern Western societies—adapting concepts derived from the study of primitive societies. The application of concepts derived from the study of relatively undifferentiated, primitive societies to highly differentiated, industrial ones such as our own facilitates the distancing which we have noted as a desideratum of many social-scientific themes. In any case some societal problems have in themselves seemed to *demand* a less culturally embedded stance; hence the attention which has been paid to pre-literate societies in the matters of population control and man/nature relationships generally, i.e. the ecological issue.

(3) Problems of Comparative Analysis in Sociology

How has comparative analysis developed in sociology? And what is its significance? In the nineteenth and early part of the twentieth centuries, there were two main forms of sociological comparison. What Nisbet calls 'the' Comparative Method, was, in the hands of its evolutionistic practitioners, little if anything more than the setting side by side of different societies and then placing them on a unilinear scale—in terms of such broad criteria as degree of cultural sophistication and degree of social differentiation.[5] In the period of Weber and Durkheim (roughly the period 1890–1920) elements of this comparative style lingered on—but in the hands of the sociologists of that time there was an injection of specialized concern with the *methodological* problems and *theoretical* implications of comparative analysis *per se*. Quite apart from the more or less technical prescriptions relating to comparative analysis which were specifically advanced by Durkheim, we see also in that same sociologist's work the beginnings of an explicit concern with the problems of social and cultural *universals*—properties which all societies may have in common. The most obviously relevant example of this preoccupation is Durkheim's thesis about the normality of crime.[6] Durkheim argued not merely that crime was inextricably a feature of the general sociocultural condition but also that it was positively functional (within limits), insofar as its occurrence and the judicial response to it served as a constant reminder of the categories of 'good' and 'bad'. This strand of Durkheim's work has not gone uncriticized, but there can be no denying that the thesis has raised crucial problems which have genuinely comparative implications. Any proposition concerning the ubiquity of a phenomenon in and of itself generates a sociological problem which can only be tackled on a comparative basis. (For example, generalizations concerning the universality of the family have raised crucial questions about the existence of different *types* of family systems and about the processes of transformation of such systems.) This is not to say, however, that generalizations about universal properties of societies, or any other kind of sociocultural collectivity, are in themselves comparative. They may merely pose problems which are capable of forming the basis for comparative inquiry. Such exercises may in fact be useful precisely because they illuminate those sociocultural phenomena

19

which are comparable and those which are not.

The outstanding comparative problems produced by Durkheim's thesis concerning the normality of crime have been, *first*, the respects in which deviance or crime rates remain relatively constant over long periods of time in particular societies or types of societies; *second*, the particular nature of this relative stability—that is, the *content* of the deviance, the kinds of deviance, and so on; and, *third*, the social and cultural processes by and through which the stability—if it obtains—is 'accomplished'.[7] Each of these three facets of the problem hypothetically involves ranges of empirical variation—variation, that is, respectively in rates (not necessarily in the empiricist 'official' crime-rate sense); deviance content; and the concrete institutional and symbolic processes of 'accomplishment'. We will have occasion at a later stage to consider the modern status, significance and ramifications of this kind of approach.

From about 1920 until as late as the early 1960's, sociologists paid relatively little attention to problems of comparison. With but a few exceptions the nearest sociologists came to comparing in any meaningful sense was the 'neutral' setting side by side of findings derived from two or more societies or smaller contexts. Comparative analysis involved, that is, merely summaries of findings in respect of different settings with little systematic attempt to pinpoint the precise nature of the similarities and dissimilarities, let alone the establishment of criteria upon which the 'comparisons' were being made. During this period a strong element of *relativism* diffused across the sociological and anthropological scenes—a development which had important implications for the study of crime and deviance generally. Societies were regarded as entities unto themselves and questions of adjudication or evaluation were ruled out of court—in sharp contrast to the eagerness of evolutionists to establish criteria of societal progress. Of course, if all social and cultural phenomena are regarded as uniquely bound together in particular societal settings—as a number of anthropologists strongly argued in the 1930's—then comparative statements even of such limited nature as 'British cities seem to be facing similar crime problems to those of America' become virtually meaningless. It should be quickly added, however, that no sociologist or anthropologist would deny the importance of 'setting' characteristics of societies, a term often used to denote the uniqueness of particular contexts.[8] But there is a considerable distance between on the one hand, the total-uniqueness view and, on the other hand, the view that every item in any given society has a parallel in other societies and that the items may be treated as if they were the same in each comparative exercise. In contemporary social science this relativism has been attenuated—although such attenuation has been less conspicuous in the study of deviance and control.

The return to comparative perspectives has been facilitated by the rapid transnationalization of social science, and a number of other factors which do not directly concern us here. Some of these new comparativists have tried to obliterate the relativity problem by returning to tenets of the unilinear evolutionists of the second half of the nineteenth century, although their approach tends to be more sophisticated, methodologically speaking, than nineteenth-century evolutionism (for example, in their inclination to use complex multi-variate statistical procedures).

Much recent comparative work, including some of the above, has operated from *objectivist* standpoints, a position which involves playing down the *subjectivity* and *culturality* of human life. These are the very facets which have been intimately studied by many of the prominent students of deviance of the past decade or so. Objectivism, as we employ the term, involves a tendency to ignore the variety of meanings attributed to everyday categories and actions both between and within societies. Those specializing in objectivist comparison tend sometimes to also overlook social-relational dynamics. Such criticisms are not intended as outright condemnations of objectivist approaches. Our point is that such should be incorporated into a wider, more comprehensive analytic context—in which individuals and groups are not merely seen as objects of inquiry but significantly as *subjects* with beliefs, values and interpretive capacities.[9]

Nevertheless there are a few specialists in the methodology of comparative research who have directly addressed the problems involved in catering for subjective and cultural factors. These factors unfortunately have been regarded by such specialists as constituting 'system interference'.[10] In effect what is sometimes being argued by the use of this phrase is that variations in situational interpretation and cultural tradition prevent relationships between 'hard' variables—for example a relationship between ethnic

21

pluralism and amount of organized crime—from being realized in all societies. Specifically, a particular cultural tradition, might 'inhibit' hypothesized consequences of ethnic pluralism. In fact many generalizing statements in sociology and political science are cast in the form: X yields Y, with the 'reservation' that cultural tradition may provide means for 'dealing' with X, of defusing its consequences. A sophisticated variation on this type of approach is provided by the work of Przeworski and Teune:

> System interference occurs when inferences from the same direct measurement statements to inferred measurement statements are not equally valid in all systems under investigation. For example, a declaration by a respondent that he would object to his son marrying an offspring of a supporter of a certain political party is not an equally valid basis in all countries for inferring 'political partisanship' defined as the 'psychological distance between or among parties'. In the United States, such an inference may be valid, while in Italy the underlying attitude may be the authoritarianism of family rather than perceived distance between parties.[11]

It is undoubtedly the case that most work on the comparative analysis of crime and deviance could be very significantly improved by operating in this manner—merely, for example, by taking variations in socio-legal norms more seriously. Such sophistication is needed merely in order to begin to make viable the kind of programme suggested in 1960 by Sheldon Glueck: a replication of researches 'designed to uncover etiologic *universals* operative as causal agents irrespective of cultural differences among the different countries'.[12] It was proposed that these studies would involve such variables as age, curves of crime, the effects of industrialization, and so on.

Such a programme is unlikely to get far without considering the validity of measuring instruments across different systems (usually societies). Most of the work done under the heading 'comparative criminology' is of the kind that *equates definitions with measurement operations*. For example, rape may be simultaneously defined and measured cross-culturally through use of 'rape' as utilized in the societies under discussion. But Przeworski and Teune's stricture points up the inadequacy of this task: 'Definitions by fiat are

22

arbitrarily true. But they are also less general'.[13] This point becomes absolutely crucial when we try to obtain *indicators* of, say, violence in a different society. In our rape example we would not employ rape as an *indicator* of any aspect of violence—for it would not be indicating, it would be defining: 'The generality of a concept does not extend beyond the results of the *particular* measuring operations'.

Such themes are central to the general problem of *equivalence* in cross-cultural research, to which it has been argued there are *technical* solutions. But such technical solutions presuppose a great deal in the form of agreement on key variables of analysis, and the danger is that we will continue to work *outwards* from the systems with which we are most familiar, 'cutting corners' dangerously as we encounter circumstances in which our starting variables do not appear in parsimonious form. Przeworski and Teune claim that the development of general, empirically-based theories is not possible in sociology except on the basis of comparative research.

The role of social science is to *explain* social events. (Our italics, RR/LT.) Explanation in comparative research is possible if and only if particular social systems observed in time and space are not viewed as definite conjunctions of constituent elements, but rather as residua of theoretical variables. General lawlike sentences can be utilized for explanatory purposes. Only if the classes of social events are viewed as generalizable beyond the limits of any particular historical social system can general lawlike sentences be used for explanation.[14]

For all its seeming attractiveness as a statement of principle this type of argument may be as methodologically premature as it is empirically constraining.

A somewhat 'softer' and more liberal view of the significance of comparative research may be found in the considerations of those like Bendix who maintain that comparative studies consist in the attempt to develop concepts and generalizations 'at a level between what is true of all societies and what is true of one society at one point in time and space'.[15] This conception is certainly much more in line with our present intentions.

We have to be highly conscious of the fact that not only etymologically and semantically, but also—much more important—cultur-

23

ally, the notions of crime and deviance vary a great deal in situational meaning as one moves from society to society. Indeed in some societies even the application of one or both of these terms may be fraught with difficulty, as we shall see more fully at a later stage in this essay. And yet at the same time it is clear that at a *sufficiently high level of abstraction*, all societies and individuals have a 'deviance problem'. There is something of a Scylla-Charybdis situation here. Adherence to Bendix's dictum about operating *between* what is true of all societies and what is true of one society clearly implies putting some rather strict limitations upon the search for equivalents in terms of high levels of abstraction. As Campbell has remarked, there are two relatively distinct levels of discourse in contemporary social science which seeks to be comparative: one that is genuinely cross-cultural and highly abstract but which is 'virtually impervious to empirical test' and a second that is empirically based but that is culturally particularistic.[16] As Frey puts it:

> the first cross-culturally-comparative-but-metaphysical level of discourse seems to be that which normally prevails at our conferences, whereas the second more often that of our empirical journal articles and academic monographs. Between the two levels is a considerable chasm.[17]

There is little point in abstraction if we end up with vacuous statements about 'everything being the same all over the world' and yet in order to begin to make analytic links between societies we have to move *in that direction*. How far we move along that path is an entirely pragmatic matter, one which can only be considered by a free-ranging inspection of many societies.

Thus we are above all concerned to introduce a form of comparative-analytic 'benchmark', some *substantive* guidelines which would allow a comparative discussion which does justice to the problems of cultural variation, subjectivity and structural dynamics.

The sociological study of crime, deviance and conformity has rarely been undertaken on such a sophisticated basis.[18] Students of such matters have not often concerned themselves in any explicit sense with the methodological problems of comparison. This is a matter for some concern in view of the rapid expansion of the study of deviant behaviour, within sociology, and of the development of comparative work in other areas of social science.

Within the study of deviance there has been a contemporary 'relativistic' stress upon fidelity to the phenomenon which has at times seemed almost incompatible with the construction of general comparative statements. David Matza has described this problem perceptively.[19] Basically, Matza favours 'naturalism' as an approach. Naturalism involves an appreciation of the richness and diversity of particular forms of deviant behaviour; it is a highly descriptive style, concerned above all with 'what actually happens'. Although attracted to some central attributes of naturalism Matza has rightly argued that the style of analysis has operated as an 'anti-philosophical philosophy'. That is, it calculatedly eschews generalizations and self-conscious attempts to systematize findings or suggest their wider implications. No philosophy, Matza argues, 'can succeed in being anti-philosophical. A counter-tendency to abstract, classify, and generalize appeared partly because it was inevitable.'[20] In other words, abstraction, classification and generalization occur whether we like them or not—and thus such exercises might as well be of as good a quality as is possible. The central question then becomes: what should these processes of abstraction, classification and generalization look like in the field in question? What, in particular, are the major analytic principles which ought to enter into studies of deviant behaviour? Having posed such questions we should quickly add that we do not thereby commit ourselves, and do certainly not try to commit all other students of deviant behaviour, to working simply and only at high levels of abstraction, in terms of complex classificatory schemes, and towards the attainment of rigidly stipulated law-like statements. Such a programme would undoubtedly stultify the analysis and discussion of the phenomenon of deviance. However, the discreteness and atomization which has marked so much of the study of deviant behaviour—even though much of that work has been highly suggestive and rich in its empirical findings—has, we maintain, to be balanced by work of a more comprehensive kind, work which takes 'the larger view' and which attempts to co-ordinate and codify discretely generated 'discoveries'.

But before we can turn to such comprehensive work, we must evaluate the strengths and weaknesses of the major existing comparative approaches to crime and deviance; in order not only that we can help to build on the strengths as we detect them but also to show the links between different kinds of standpoint.

25

(B) DEFICIENCIES OF COMPARATIVE RESEARCH ON DEVIANCE AND SOCIAL CONTROL

The studies discussed here are chosen for consideration not so much because of their basic subject matter—juvenile delinquency in Eastern Europe, corruption in developing societies—but rather because they are illustrative of distinctive conceptual and methodological problems. We are not, in any sense, therefore, engaged in producing empirical generalizations or conclusions. Such a procedure would not only conflict with our purposes but would also in some way negate them, for a large part of our argument is that many findings covering two or more settings must be regarded as illegitimate on the grounds that they have issued from dissimilar modes of inquiry. Our concern with procedural problems rather than empirical findings has also led us to include some material which is not explicitly comparative.

We initiate this survey by considering in a deliberately naïve manner the problems of selection which face a social scientist who, seeking to establish some modest empirical cross-cultural generalizations, sets out to study crime and deviance phenomena in a number of different societies. We will not endow him with any ambitious notions about the wider significance of his work.

How will he proceed? For a start he must have definitions of 'crime' and 'deviance'. We will take the simplest course and provide him with conventional sociological definitions. According to these '*crime* is that behaviour which violates the criminal law' and '*deviance* is that behaviour which violates community social norms to such an extent as to elicit indications of disapproval or negative sanctions'.[1]

There will of course be a variety of arguments which he will have to resolve about marginal cases, arguments which suggest that this or that type of behaviour should be firmly included or excluded (depending upon the argument) from the 'criminal' category. He will feel some uncertainty about the degree of disapproval which is a precondition for asserting the presence of deviance, or about the degree of generality which should be involved in the specification of 'community'.

These problems are in no way insurmountable. Certain types of behaviour unambiguously violate the criminal law and others bring clear indications of strong disapproval from the community in which they take place. The criminologist who is studying a single society or segment thereof can proceed at this point to relate such relatively unambiguous criminality or deviance to other examples of crime and deviance, or to other aspects of social life with which he believes they enjoy a relationship. He may for example study the link between dangerous driving and drinking, or between bank-robbery and technological advances in security measures. His critics may attack the statistics upon which he relies and the conclusions which he draws but the validity of the enterprise is rarely questioned.

Our *comparative* criminologist's problems are however only beginning at this point. The relatively unambiguous location of examples of criminal or deviant behaviour in one society provides no automatic warrant for taking them out of their domestic contexts and juxtaposing them against other phenomena in different societies. For such elements as 'drinking' and 'dangerous driving' are not independent items like rocks and stones and should not therefore be prised from their surroundings, conclusively labelled and transported happily across the seas for comparison with other similarly documented examples. 'Dangerous driving' and 'drinking' are items in a particular language of meaning—they are not merely words which are tied on to clearly identifiable pieces of behaviour. We know what 'dangerous driving' means not simply because we understand by the dictionary meaning of each word—know for example that 'dangerous' is the opposite of safe, that 'driving' is the name of a skill comparable to cycling—but because we have ideas about the nature of responsibility on the roads, about the precedence which should be given to humans over machines. 'Dangerous driving' is a concept whose full meaning is dependent upon a set of assumptions about the value of human life, about an individual's right to have protection from others who threaten him. Similarly 'drinking' involves not just a reference to the consumption of liquid but to a set of norms about the use of alcohol

27

in social life. When a criminologist working within one context links these two phenomena together he is relating concepts which are already in the same universe of discourse. They belong to the same cultural context; those who know the norms and values which surround driving upon the road will also be acquainted with those which relate to the consumption of alcohol. We therefore know what the criminologist is about when he relates such items. We allow that these are appropriate phenomena to be considered together by virtue of their both being connected to a single normative framework. This is not to pre-judge their inter-relationship— but only to suggest that the *consideration* of such a relationship is given a warranty by the general recognition of the common cultural context from which the items are drawn.

The comparative criminologist has no such warranty for the comparison of behavioural phenomena drawn from one society with those of another. It is not simply that he may have language translation difficulties, but he will also be handicapped by lack of familiarity with the situational meanings which operate within different societies. He has a double translation problem. He has not simply to find a linguistic equivalent of 'dangerous driving' and 'drinking' in another society but he has to find two comparable elements which are normatively related to each other in similar ways.

There is a further problem for the comparative criminologist in that the object of his attention—crime and deviance—is not unambiguously located within one system of meaning.

While there may be a common cultural system which gives meaning to both criminal and deviant behaviour, criminal acts are both distinctively conceptualized by the criminals themselves and by agents of social control, whose act of legislation may have made the behaviour criminal in the first place or who may now be charged with apprehending and sanctioning those who engage in it. Within such alternative meaning systems, particular acts of deviance may lose their popular meaning. An act of dangerous driving may be 'only a statistic' within one meaning system, whereas within another it may be 'the only way to get home quickly' and within another 'a typical Saturday night offence'. This relativization of the meaning of the behaviour does not change its total character. The deviant himself, the official statistician and the policeman, may all be fully agreed about the illegality of the act but

28

they will—because of having conceived it within a different meaning system—hold different views about its general significance, about its seriousness.

This elaboration of the cultural entanglements within which crime and deviance are embedded may engender pessimism about the whole idea of comparative work. But the presence of different meaning systems may actually give us some additional comparative leverage. For it enables us to compare not only crime and deviance but the variety of meaning systems within which they are located in different societies. For in many societies we will find that there are restrictions upon the number of meaning systems within which particular concepts may be located. The distinction between the public and private conception of a crime may for example not exist, the deviant may fully concur with the descriptions and accounts of his behaviour which are provided by his judges who in turn articulate their conception of the behaviour not from the standpoint of the distinctive meaning system of an agent of social control but in terms which are elements in a common cultural system. Whereas, in our society we are used to situations in which crimes repeatedly change their meaning as they are publicly shifted from one cultural domain to another by prisoners, judges and journalists, in other societies such debates will be more or less inconceivable by virtue of the homogeneity of the cultural system. But this cultural differentiation not only relativizes the behaviour under consideration, it is also itself relative. It is a *variable* characteristic of human societies.

The comparative criminologist will encounter cases in which the meaning of a particular act is the object of considerable conflict by adherents of different meaning systems, as when particular deviants consistently contradict police or judicial definitions of their behaviour as anti-social or criminal. In these circumstances the need to take the cultural embeddedness of the phenomenon into account when moving to comparative work would not be met by a display of sensitivity towards one system of meaning. It would not for example be appropriate in many contemporary industrial societies to take homosexuality as merely part of a range of sexual offences which were regarded by social controllers as indicative of abnormal psychological functioning and as threats to the 'moral fibre of the nation'. Homosexuality is also considered by articulate sections of society to be meaningfully compatible with progressive

29

liberal ideas about sexual relations. The presence of this alternative conception changes the actual meaning of the behaviour for some if not all who engage in it. A clear alternative meaning system is available to them for reference and this not only affects the reasons for their decision to engage in the behaviour but also their attitudes to arrest and punishment following it. The very act becomes different because of its potential incorporation within two meaning systems. To insist that the behaviour is still really the same is to indulge in a form of essentialism.

We are arguing that criminologists are often allowed to propose relationships between patterns of behaviour in their own country without being questioned about the assumptions which lie behind their choice of behaviours because we 'know what they mean'— we fill the unexplained gaps in their research with our own common-sense knowledge. But when comparative work is undertaken the cultural relativity of this common-sense becomes very evident. We can no longer ignore the sociocultural embeddedness of deviance and social control. But as we have begun to argue already this is not equivalent to adopting a completely relativistic position.

Satisfactory comparative work on crime and deviance also demands a de-reification of the notion of social control. Many studies of deviance are conceived in terms of a straightforward conflict between the criminal and the forces of law and order. Judges, policemen, statisticians and probation officers, are all assumed to be united in their beliefs about the need to reduce crime even if they differ occasionally in their methods. An assumption of the homogeneity of values between agents of social control helps to maintain the myth of a central unitary concept of justice. It reinforces the view of the law as an element which stands outside the actual activities of human beings. But of course, not only are there important differences in the way in which law is interpreted by different agents of social control, but there are very significant differences in the degree of legitimacy which is accorded to certain aspects of it by different groups of social controllers. The police will not only have a distinctive way of interpreting the laws on sexual offenders and dangerous driving, they will also place a distinctive value upon the significance of violations of such laws. Comparative work which is based upon a view of law as a transcendent entity to which all non-deviants orient in a unitary fashion is as

30

barren as comparative work which assumes crime to be a residual pathological entity which disgusts all good men the world over.

(1) *Statistical Approaches to Comparison*

With these reservations in mind, we can begin to appraise some comparative studies of crime and deviance. The initial interest in comparative studies of crime was part of the general positivistic search in the nineteenth century for regularities in the rates of various social phenomena.[2] Thus Adolphe Quetelet drew upon statistical material from French and Belgian sources in order to assert that the volume and kind of crime in any particular country remained remarkably constant over time. As long as the basic institutions of society—economic, social, political—remained stable then this constant characteristic of crime would obtain. Crime was endemic to society—it was one of the tolls that had to be paid—'un budget qu'on paie avec une regularité effrayante'.[3] In exercises such as those conducted by Quetelet there was no concern with meaningfully equating the criminal behaviour in one society with that which occurred in another. The belief in social regularities was subscribed to with sufficient fervour to make a concern with the nature of crime of only passing interest. The rates told their own story; they were the 'reality', there was no need to refer any further to the behaviour which they described. Durkheim, at least recognized the inadequacy of this approach in his study of suicide. For him, there was a reality that underpinned the rates themselves. While the statistics for suicide like those for murder studied by Quetelet showed a constancy when specific periods within one society were examined, there were clear differences over time and between societies, and Durkheim argued that it was the sociologist's task to examine the basis for the differential suicide 'budget' which had to be paid in such differing circumstances. He consequently explored variations in underlying social reality that produced different types of suicide. In fact he distinguished types of suicide precisely according to the social causes which could be said to be operating in different societal contexts, although not according to any distinctive characteristics of the suicide act itself. 'We shall be able', he wrote, 'to determine the

31

social types of suicide by clarifying them not directly by their preliminary described characteristics, but by the causes which produce them ... In a word instead of being morphological, our clarification will from the start be ethnological. Nor is this a sign of inferiority, for the nature of a phenomenon is much more profoundly got at by knowing its cause, than by knowing its characteristics only, even the essential ones'.[4]

Durkheim's more sophisticated approach to the nature of deviant behaviour was mitigated by necessary reliance upon inadequate statistics. This is a common problem in comparative analysis. Readers of introductory text-books on criminology will be familiar —perhaps over-familiar— with the standard ways of throwing doubt upon statistical enterprises.[5] In the first place the reliability of the statistics is questioned: they are declared to be only a sample of the amount of crime within any one country—a biased sample in that they record the number of crimes 'cleared up' or 'reported' rather than the actual number committed. It is pointed out that the size and representativeness of the sample is not in any case constant across the different categories of crime. So the number of murders 'cleared up' and reported in the statistics bears a specific proportionate relationship to the whole number of cases of that crime, a proportionate relationship which does not hold for other categories of crime. One in every three murders may be reported but only one in every five thousand cases of illegal abortion may come to police attention. This problem of hidden crime is difficult enough to deal with in a domestic statistical survey in view of differential regional emphasis upon the importance of clearing up particular types of crime. It is compounded when cross-cultural analysis is attempted, when wholly different national attitudes to such matters as interpersonal violence and deviant sexual behaviour are somewhere hidden behind the size of the figure which is handed to the international agency concerned with comparison.

Even if we could adequately determine the size of the sample of actual crime which was represented by the statistic, we would be in no position to treat figures from different societies as truly comparable data. For apart from their lack of reliability, there are also questions about their validity. When we begin to unpack such terms as fraud, sexual offences and larceny we find that they do not refer to a clearly identified, readily circumscribed behaviour. They are not sociological categories with pretensions to universality but

32

rather legal or statistical categories which reflect historical and contemporary attitudes toward particular behaviour in their titles—fraud, embezzlement, grand larceny, dangerous driving—and in their differentiation—misdemeanours and felonies, indictable and non-indictable. Cressey is amongst those sociologists who have argued that a necessary precondition for comparison is the use of sociological categories which transcend such categorical relativity by using clear behavioural similarities as criteria for inclusion. When he conducted his inquiry into embezzlement he became aware that the 'legal category did not describe a homogeneous class of criminal behaviour' and therefore produced an alternative categorization in order to proceed with his etiological investigation.[6] This scepticism about the value of legal categories must not however be taken too far. The fact of their relativity does not exclude them from use by the sociologist. Studies of the way in which legal categories of crime *are* used by agents of social control tell us a great deal about the sets of assumptions about the offender, the offence and the community, which are held by their users.[7]

In recent years the criticism of those who rely on surface, official statistical data has become more sophisticated. The traditional concerns about the reliability and validity of the activity remain, but in addition attention has been paid to the ways in which sets of statistics are actually assembled by various agents of social control. Aaron Circourel in his pioneering comparative study of delinquency rates took two cities, A and B, and examined their police and probation files.[8] Initially he examined the statistical rates in the manner usually adopted by social scientists, that is in line with the practice of using statistical rates *disengaged* from the everyday practices of the organizations producing them. In doing so he is able to point to major discrepancies between the different city rates. For example there was a *large* discrepancy between the number of apprehensions of criminals despite the almost identical social composition of the populations of both cities; similarly differences between the two in the rates for petty theft and car theft were difficult to understand by reference to the composition of the two cities. Neither could the differences be adequately accounted for by reference to differential police efficiency.[9] The presence of these discrepancies, argues Circourel, compels the researcher to pay attention to the way in which the police decide to include or exclude certain types of behaviour in relation to particular categories. 'The nego-

33

tiable character of what is going on must not be underestimated by the "solid" appearing nature of the categories and numbers.'[10]

The rest of Circourel's study is concerned with establishing the nature of this negotiation, the everyday decision making which produces the figures. The processes which underlie the 'accomplishment' of rates are in no way random. They can be traced to what Circourel calls 'the organizational influences of day-to-day policy implementation'. These different organizational policies as interpreted by officers on the spot dealing with cases 'directly changed the size of the "law-enforcement net" for recognizing and processing juveniles viewed as delinquent, and determined the size and conception of the "social problem"'.[11] Valid comparison should then involve not just a comparison of the assembled rates, but a comparison of the different organizational policies which underlie them *and* of the practices adopted by police and others when they come to deal with actual cases. This means that statements such as 'Nigeria is beginning to show an increase in delinquency' or 'in West Africa, juvenile delinquency is almost non-existent as a problem' (and we quote from a recently published cross-cultural survey) retain their interest not so much as inviolable statements about trends in different cultures, but rather as indicating the presence of an opportunity to examine the ways in which delinquency rates are assembled in different cultural contexts.[12] At least this is true of the present situation. Obviously there could be circumstances where due attention had been given to such matter in the construction of comparative statements and where generalizations derived from assembled figures might therefore be treated as sociologically meaningful.

The limits upon types of conclusions which can be reached at the moment by the use of comparative statistics are well illustrated in a recent study by Wolf.[13] Wolf is a sophisticated criminologist, recognizing that the mere juxtaposition of national criminal data is a meaningless exercise in the present circumstances. The figures of reported crimes which are available for different societies at the moment must be considered 'the resultants of an interplay in each country between various factors such as the actual criminality, the legal depictions, the tolerance level of the general population (readiness to report crimes to the authorities), the efficiency of the police force and judicial authorities, as well as that of statistical bureaux etc.'[14] Nevertheless Wolf suggests that the reported figures may still

34

be used to indicate relationships between total crime rates and the increasing developmental status of a country. The figures also indicate changes in the *ratio* of the number of reported murders per 100,000 population to the number of reported larcenies per 100,000. This ratio appears to decrease with increasing social and economic development. These appear relatively insignificant findings when placed alongside some of the deductions of the earlier statistically minded comparative criminologists, although they are based upon considerably more comprehensive and sophisticated statistical reports. The problem which bedevils statistical approaches is that each improvement in the collection of data is undermined by a new sociological critique of the basis upon which such data is collected. The comparative criminologist who is aware of both aspects is therefore forced to confine himself to the type of modest generalizations which form the conclusions of Wolf's study.

In our earlier discussion we concentrated upon the significance of meaning in comparative studies. Statistical studies are often literally meaningless. Larceny and murder in different societies are given no especial significance beyond the indications of their incidence contained in the figures relating to them. How can we bring them into any useful correspondence if this remains the case? As Merton asks 'Is one homicide to be equated with ten petty thefts? 100? 1,000? We may sense that these are incommensurables and so feel that the question of comparing their magnitude is a nonsense question. Yet this feeling is only a prelude to recognition of the more general fact that we have no strict common denominator for social problems and so have no workable procedures for comparing the scale of different problems, even when the task is simplified by dealing with two kinds of criminal act.'[15] It is this fairly fundamental recognition of the need to take some account of meaning—fundamental in that the meaning which is considered by Merton is confined to such matters as the significance of the crime to the community or the 'general public'—that has led to research upon the construction of indexes of crime.

Wolfgang and Sellin have suggested ways in which offences might be compared not simply by contrasting gross rates but by matching totals according to the relative seriousness of the compared offences.[16] Their system was devised by giving carefully prepared accounts of different crimes to three samples of people—policemen, university students and juvenile court judges. These accounts

35

included such elements as death of the victim, use of weapon, value of property stolen. The weighting was calculated from the points rating given from the various accounts. Once this weighting system is available, it becomes possible to compare communities not in terms of the actual offences committed but in terms of the relative seriousness of the crimes which were reported in each locality. But whilst such a system gains information in one respect (i.e. in terms of providing a quantified guide to seriousness) it loses it in another. Nigel Walker's example makes this criticism clear. He hypothesizes a case in which the index for Sodom in 1970 might be 117,634 while for Gomorrah it might be 219,839, for the same towns in 1975 it might be 128,000 and 213,111 respectively. 'What is not made clear is in what way this would be an improvement on the crude system of counting each reported crime as one. It might appear to tell us that Gomorrah had a more serious crime problem than Sodom (assuming the two towns to be of comparable size), but it would not tell us whether this was because Gomorrah's crimes included more murders, personal violence and the use of weapons, or because it included a very large number of lucrative thefts, burglaries and frauds.'[17] Walker might also have stressed not only the loss of information involved in the use of the Wolfgang and Sellin index but also the complexity involved in recording the differing seriousness ratings over time and for the different populations involved.

The significance of contemporary critiques of orthodox statistical measurement of the incidence of crime is not adequately conveyed if one simply regards them as proposing a set of new variables which must be taken into account in the compilation of quantitative data. Neither is it enough to allow that they also draw attention to the meaning of particular laws to those who are engaged in enforcing them. The principal significance of such critiques of most statistical work lies in their appreciation of the *negotiated* character of deviance. This stress is antithetical to the more objectivist emphasis which informs most statistical studies. Crime no longer becomes an entity which is to be put down, to be counted, to be pushed around for inspection—it is no longer separated from the agents of social control—instead it is seen as only capable of being 'realized' in an important sense through the active work of such agents. As McHugh observes: 'To note and count the inhabitants of these tables (i.e. statistical and summary tables RR/LT) as deviant is to accede to common-sense judgments already made, not to describe those judgments while being made, and of which the inhabitants are mere traces'.[18] The forces of law and order are not so much at war with the deviants as involved with individuals in a variety of negotiations with differential outcomes for both parties. Once this perspective is adopted the aims and intentions of the deviants become significant. Questions about the cause of their behaviour (which implicitly inform most comparative statistical work) have less significance than statements which do justice to its nature. Cicourel's improvement upon the simplistic social-control approach which informs objectivist accounts of deviance is not unexpected when viewed against the dominant emphases within the sociology of deviance in the United States in the last twenty years. It is the comparative significance of this work which we must now consider.

(2)   The Problem of Conceptual Diffusion

Although the social control perspective has dominated comparative statistical studies it has been noticeably absent from much of the sociological work on deviant behaviour. Policemen, judges and magistrates make only token appearances in the work of the sub-cultural theorists and in the later work of the labelling theorists they only make a brief entry in order to set into motion the reactive consequence with which the theorist is concerned.[19] But this new form of one-sidedness is at least partly redressed by the sociologists' typical determination to establish the distinctive characteristics of a range of deviant behaviour. When the subcultural theorists turn their attention to violence and vandalism, they re-interpret the phenomena; they translate it from a statisic into an activity which can only be comprehended by relating it to a cultural and structural context. Cohen's vandals are not just deviants, they are necessarily working class, American educational failures; these are the characteristics which give meaning to their behaviour.[20] This concern with cultural specificity creates serious problems for the comparative analyst. Concepts like sub-culture, social disorganization, and opportunity structure which are coined in specific contexts to give meaning to observed behaviour are not immediately translatable

37

to other environments. Not that this has prevented the often crude transplantation of such concepts to other cultures. The problem is that the greatest concentration of social scientists in the area of crime and deviance is to be found in that society which is thought in simplistic terms to have the 'highest rates' and the 'greatest problem'—that is, the United States.

The effect of this concentration of academic resources can be seen in many of those so-called cross-cultural studies in which deviant phenomena in societies other than the United States (and perhaps Great Britain) are tentatively harnessed to the conceptual and theoretical apparatus which has been assembled by social scientists in those countries.[21] So we may find scholars demonstrating the similarity between street gangs in their native country and the United States. 'Subcultures' will allegedly be detected in Hong Kong; 'violent gangs' will emerge in Paris; 'organized crime' will be found in Accra. Of course, one assumption of comparative analysis is that there will indeed be equivalent forms of deviance appearing in societies which share structural and cultural characteristics, which are at similar stages in industrialization, urbanization and so on. But at the moment, the overpowering conceptual edifice of American criminology, coupled of course with the international prestige which accumulates to its utilizers, means that investigators of what to us are distant societies find their way into the problem area of deviance through concepts developed in culturally alien contexts. There may be a certain appropriateness in examining aspects of juvenile delinquency which appear to be the result of cultural diffusion by means of the tools which have been used for their analysis in their society of origin, but the unlikelihood of such simple transference or replication of deviant phenomena has been adequately highlighted in one of the rare pieces of extended comparative work on subcultures, namely Downes' study of delinquent subcultures in the East End of London.[22] Perhaps the saddest example which we have encountered of a 'parasitic' comparative study was written by two Indians who attempted to apply the findings from overcrowding in the United States to the figures for delinquency in Calcutta. The variable which proved difficult to accommodate was that it was not just houses in Calcutta which were overcrowded with residents but also pavements.

It should be said at this juncture that specialists in comparative analysis have paid considerable attention to some of the issues
38

raised by the problem of diffusion.[23] This has not involved so much the question of the diffusion of social scientific concepts but, as in the case which we have mentioned concerning juvenile delinquency, the diffusion of beliefs and values in the real world. The distinction between analytic concepts and phenomenal beliefs and values is crucial—for unless there is clear-cut evidence of concrete beliefs and values either being indigenous to a particular setting or having been diffused into it, then ready application of concepts derived from a 'distant' source is fraught with difficulty. The major contribution which has been made to this kind of problem has to do with what is known as Galton's Problem: how do we decide whether the presence of an item in a particular context is the consequence of diffusion from another context or has been generated through functional interdependence with other items? One such empirical problem has concerned slavery in the USA—an argument between those who see major features of American slavery as having been diffused from the African origins of slaves and those who see those features as having been wrought in the process of master-slave relationships. It is unlikely that many problems can be analysed exclusively in terms of *one* of these standpoints: diffusion and internal generation are not mutually exclusive processes. But sensitivity to the methodological problems enhances our comprehension of deviance and crime phenomena and might dampen down the tendency to vacillate wildly between attributing crime tendencies in Britain to 'Americanization', on the one hand, and deficiencies of British society, on the other. Cressey, for example, has shown how both in analytic and in lay terms much misunderstanding can be created in attributing to British society a problem of organized crime.[24] As a characterization of certain developments in crime performed by groups on a regular basis it is misleading, if the intention is to say that it is similar to that which is called organized crime in America. As a form of comprehension it is misleading because it often implies that it 'came straight from America'. Both of these views can be strongly challenged on empirical grounds and both certainly neglect the intricacies of the diffusion *versus* internal-generation problem.

Few books have been published by sociologists which devote themselves *explicitly* to cross-cultural problems in the analysis of deviance. Cavan and Cavan have produced one of the best known of these.[25] This, for all its commendable intentions, turns out to consist of little more than sketches of particular societies in terms of such variables as degree of industrialization, history of social conflict and approximate stage of development. Once the societies have been characterized, then their general or specific crime rates are produced and some interpretive links are attempted. At least here we find some sensitivity to distinctive *forms* of deviance. The authors have assembled material on delinquency in twelve countries. The limitations of the studies they have assembled however restricts them to making general statements about the higher rates which accompany the 'breakdown of traditional patterns of social organization'. They are forced to work with global assumptions, to construct correlations between 'social problems' without having any opportunity to examine the ways in which significance has become attached to such conduct. Their reliance upon American influenced secondary sources means that they tend to arrive at statements such as: 'At present, city delinquency, like much of city life itself, is in a rudimentary stage of development. It grows out of poverty, dire need, and lack of social organization in the slums.' The value of such statements is readily undermined by contrasting them with the findings of an anthropologist, who, unfamiliar with deviance theory, simply sets out to describe delinquency in one African city.[26] There, the researcher found not only a definite urban tradition, but also a high degree of social organization, a deviant population whose political involvement paralleled that in some American cities, and a culture of deviance which syncretically involved witchcraft elements and contemporary advertising themes.

The assumptions which lie behind the work of the Cavans are nevertheless much less disconcerting from a comparative standpoint than those which have informed other recent comparative work. One author introduces his text by the following statement of his belief: 'Allowing for some cultural, economic or politically imposed differences, "delinquent behaviour" is expressed in the same way and causes the same reactions in all countries where the lives of people are ruled by the values and techniques of modern industrial society'.[27] Needless to say, the writer does not describe the way in which such differences may be conceptualized; we are not told the way in which they can be peeled off so as to reveal beneath their surface the homogenous cultural phenomenon of contemporary delinquency. But then the book from which we quote is, like many others, an advertisement for a particular correctional

40

method. We need to be aware, in assessing the reliability of particular cross-cultural analysis, of the advantages which may ensue for social practitioners if they can show that deviant phenomena in other societies are directly comparable to the domestic variety and, therefore, by definition are amenable to tried, trusted and institutionalized correctional techniques.

This discussion of the dangers of conceptual diffusion was related to the work of those sociologists of deviance who put on one side the nature of social control and concentrated upon the structural and cultural factors which gave particular forms of crime and deviance their distinctive meaning. Our reservations about this type of approach in comparative work relate only to the export of concepts derived from it and not to the actual viability of the *approach*. Subcultural theory or social disorganization theory may prove to be an appropriate way of summarizing findings outside the United States; what cannot be *assumed*, however, is that the characteristics of subcultures which have been delineated by American researchers are likely to be replicated in different societies.

(3) *Ethnographic Approaches*

If problems of translation and methodological adaptation are difficult in the area of subcultural theory, they are compounded by the more ethnographic type of analysis which is now favoured by several prominent sociologists of deviance. The ethnographers share with earlier theorists a lack of concern for the nature and varieties of social control. Their concern is with the meaning of deviance to the deviant in tightly circumscribed contexts. General concepts are distrusted in that they are thought to violate the distinctiveness of particular deviant enterprises. The injunction is to approach the deviant world with an especial sensitivity, with a real sense of trying to appreciate the phenomenon. In this way the deviant enterprise may not simply be seen as lacking pathological characteristics but it may also be seen as perfectly 'natural'. The favoured technique is that of participant observation and generalizations are eschewed. The characteristics of the hustlers studied by Ned Polsky, or of the closet-queens observed by Laud Humphreys are not even proposed as generalizable to other contexts within the United

States, even less are they offered as typifications which might have relevance to hustling or homosexuality within different societies.[28] The full attention and sensitivity of the ethnographer is devoted to 'getting matters right' in his own context.

Lee Rainwater in commenting upon Humphrey's study hopes that 'its results will encourage sociologists to seek out other unstructured collectivities of persons engaged in deviant behaviour, to study how that behaviour is organized and sustained with minimal subcultural supports, and why',[29] Elsewhere he talks about the need for 'systematic comparisons between the situations of hobbyists whose hobbies are legal (like fishermen, hunters or photographers) and those whose hobbies are shady (sexual deviants, drug users, pornography consumers, weekend hippies, and the like)'.[30] These comparative hopes are however far from being realized by sociologists of deviance. At the moment the dissatisfaction with the character of pre-existing generalizations about deviant behaviour amongst ethnographers continues to produce a hyper-involvement with the affairs of specific cultures.

The contemporary approaches to crime and deviance which we have been considering have appeared unlikely to generate satisfactory comparative research because of their over-emphasis upon the 'unique' qualities of deviant phenomena, and/or because of their relative neglect of the nature of social control.

(4)   The Evolution of Social Control

It is this latter aspect which receives extensive treatment in a variety of comparative historical studies of an 'evolutionary' character. These concentrate in their analysis upon changes in the nature of social control, but tend to regard deviance as a relatively constant phenomenon—at least qualitatively. The argument (by default usually) is that the nature of deviant behaviour does not change greatly in a diachronic perspective—men still want to engage in distinctive types of sexual behaviour, to steal, to murder. What changes are the *ways* in which such behaviour is dealt with by society. It is argued that crime is a permanent problem in human society and that our attention should be directed to the ways in which it was confronted at different times. In some such developmental accounts we may find descriptions of periods which are said to be filled with excessive violence or a particular blood-thirstiness. This promises a description of deviant behaviour but on examination these qualities turn out to be not characteristics of the deviants— but rather of the agents of social control. In classical 'evolutionary' treatment of comparative criminal law, we are confronted with the gradual emergence of a particular view of punishment. Hobhouse, for example, declared that the object of his major work is 'to trace the evolution of the ethical consciousness as displayed in the habits and customs, rules and principles, which have arisen in the course of human history for the regulation of human conduct'.[31] Comparative studies of deviance of an evolutionary or 'progressive' kind have often not merely ignored the possibility of differences in the meaning of the deviant act itself, but also in the meaning of the sanctions which are directed against the act. Hobhouse merely talks of severe punishment characterizing certain periods. The exact meaning of the sanctions is no more investigated than the exact meaning of the behaviour against which they are directed. This or that sanction is merely accorded an ethical score on the continuum from barbarism to liberality. Other writers who have had a less linear and evaluative conception of changes in the nature of social control, have concentrated instead upon developments of legal norms but have still hardly paid attention to the nature of the behaviour to which the law is addressed. Instead the relationships studied have been between law and other major aspects and institutions of society. Maine related the rise of contract to the declining role of kinship; Durkheim related the move from repressive to restitutive sanctions to the growth of the division of labour.

More recently, we find the study of legal evolution by Richard Schwartz and James Miller which draws upon cross-cultural material in the Human Area Relation files to demonstrate that legal characteristics occur in a standard sequential order.[32] These authors do at least admit that there are practical reasons for concentrating upon certain societal features rather than others:

No effort is made to observe the presence of such important phenomena as respect for the law, the use of generalized norms and the pervasiveness of deviance—induced disturbance. Although all of these should be included in a comprehensive theory of legal evolution, they are omitted here in the interest of

43

observational reliability.[33]

One of the very few counter-examples to this tendency to over-concentrate upon the 'legal side' amongst developmentally-oriented students of crime, is provided by Nils Christie.[34] Christie argues that it may be misleading to rely upon the means of punishment as a social indicator for it may be that changes in such means are related not to some ongoing, even evolutionary, tendency to liberalization or humanitarianism, but are rather related to the nature of the crime to which they are addressed. It could in other words be 'the values that are destroyed or violated by misdeeds which have changed over time and not the values which inform the punishment'.[35] Unfortunately, as he observes, we do not, like the economists, have a golden yardstick against which we can measure changes in the value of crime and punishment. Indeed Christie is forced to admit that we cannot easily discover whether the values actually violated by criminals are now of more or less central societal significance than at other historical times. He nevertheless suggests by reference to crimes concerned with material gain that 'crimes are considered as about equally grave evils now as before, and that it is therefore the penal values—not the crime values—that have changed'.[36] This admittedly speculative conclusion which ignores the changing meaning of crime by concentrating upon the economic compatibility of the criminal's gain and the victim's loss over time, at least allows him to proceed to a viable empirical study of possible changes in penal values.

Such perspectives as those described above tend then to concentrate upon changes in penal values, they do not seriously discuss changes in the nature of crime; crime is very much the independent variable which remains uniform, but which by its continued presence provokes a series of reactions which can then be taken as indicative of the general values prevailing at the time. An evolutionary approach by Yehudi Cohen interestingly departs from this position by concentrating upon the deviant behaviour not as some constant element which inevitably provokes some reaction—but by viewing the behaviour as varying in the extent to which it is tolerable within particular types of society.[37] Again the behaviour is assumed to be constant, to have the same nature; it means much the same to the members of society but it has a differing meaning at different periods for political and legal élites and it is this rather than any

44

changes in penal values *per se* which is responsible for temporally differentiated responses. The differing social reactions to the deviant behaviour do not ensure that the meaning of the behaviour is thereby changed for the individuals who are engaged in it or who are tempted to be so. According to this perspective it is not possible to make inferences about people's personal motivations from a knowledge of formal or informal sanctions. Cohen invokes research in a highland Jamaican community to justify such a position. Research into this community, which was characterized by permissive sexual norms, showed that the anxieties experienced there in relation to sex hardly differed from those experienced by people who had been socialized in more restrictive Western circumstances. This is an ethnographic 'put-down' which is necessary if Cohen is to maintain his evolutionary stance.[38] For, to allow that the deviant act changes its actual meaning over time, to allow that the motivations which inform it vary, or that the objects of its attention shift is to blur the mainline evolutionary posture. We can observe a shift in ethical stance, in penal values or moral progress as long as the eliciting object 'stays still'. Cohen does not want to talk about penal values or moral progress but about different styles of political control. He explores the way in which the rulers of some nations 'achieve some of their political ends by imposing unique controls over sexual behaviour'. The research uses a sample of sixty cultures selected from Murdock's World Ethnographic sample and does not, like many similar anthropological enterprises, stop at a comparison of traditional societies but goes on to propose an explanation for the contemporary political tolerances of sexual deviance which has interesting—if unacknowledged—affinities with the idea of state relaxation for definite goals that lies behind the Marcusian conception of repressive desublimation. It is, in other words, a comparative study of the political response to one form of deviance which has something to say about the nature of the contemporary reaction to such deviance.

There are two important differences between the evolutionary-comparative perspective which we have just discussed and that adopted by Marc Ancel.[39] The first is in the nature of the treatment of deviant behaviour. Ancel's concerns are sufficiently close to everyday social problems to allow him to recognize the fact that an increasingly wide variety of acts are declared deviant by the state. It becomes difficult to regard crime as a behavioural constant

45

when one is faced with such relatively diverse and novel behaviour as vandalism, industrial sabotage and football hooliganism. Ancel does not therefore record the ways in which the law responds to supposedly homogenous and traditional deviant phenomena like incest, adultery or homosexuality and from this infer changes in the goals of the state from variations in state response. Instead he concentrates upon the changing nature of the response to particular deviant acts. He is thus led to conclude that we can no longer talk in terms of absolutes when discussing the nature of politico-social control. Law now takes into account a wide variety of extra-legal considerations in determining the response to particular forms of deviance. The behaviour may be seen as threatening at one time and therefore incurring severe penalties; at another time, however, it may be assumed to be mere evidence of individualized pathology and so be dealt with more tolerantly. The deviant behaviour thus acquires some meaning, and responses to it can only be understood in terms of this meaning. However, the meaning is not the meaning attached to it by the actor but that given to it by the law—it represents an evaluation by the judge of its 'dangerousness'. A second disinguishing mark of this evolutionary comparative position is introduced by Ancel's stress upon the self-consciousness which is implied by the move from formal penal codes with absolute prohibitions to a situation in which particular behaviour is readily reacted to in a pragmatic way by a legal authority, which contemporaneously defines it as deviant.

Ancel is anxious not merely to record evolutionary trends in the nature of social control; he is specifically concerned with making certain evolutionary tendencies explicit for lawyers and politicians, so that the law can be given a more fundamentally creative role in social and political matters. One has to capitalize on the evolutionary tendencies. One must for this purpose look at 'the whole panorama of European codification in its dynamic evolutions'.[40] One perceives then that this evolution is in reality necessitated by new forces, be they unionism, socialism, state control, or concern for protecting the family, youth and public morality. 'Once more, the weak structure of legalism breaks under the pressure of impelling forces, but these now come from a new conception of criminal policy.'[41] The significance of the present evolutionary phase for Ancel is that our attention can now shift from the traditional concern with rules—with the absolutes which were incorporated in different penal codes—and look instead at the specific responses of a given society to the phenomenon of crime; pure legalism is on the retreat, the law is now being used quite self-consciously for the realization of certain social needs and concerns.

The 'de-legalization' advocated by the social defence movement involves a struggle against excessive legalism (juridisme) which by relying on fictions and purely abstract forms of reasoning, often threatens to conceal the real nature of crime and the criminal.[42]

The persistent tendency in most of the evolutionary approaches we have described is the imposition of a relatively homogeneous character upon deviant behaviour. Diversity, change and development are looked for in areas of penal values, social control and judicial process.

(5)   What is the Unit of Comparison?

The problem of what ought to be compared has already been raised in this discussion and we have been critical of those studies—such as the statistical ones—which relied upon units of comparison whose nature was so limited as to preclude any attribution of meaning. But exactly how 'general' should our unit of comparison be if we are to do justice to the meaningful context in which it is embedded? It will be useful to give an example from a study of homicide and suicide in Africa. The author of this study, Bohannan, starts by attacking theorists such as Durkheim who he declares used inappropriate items for comparison.[43] The comparison of rates, he argues, tells us nothing about the system of meaning within which the act is located. How may we expand the unit to deal with this problem? Bohannan suggests that we should first of all elicit the reasons for the homicide or suicide by questioning surviving kinsmen. These reasons are not the new units of comparison— Bohannan is not proposing a comparative study of the motives for suicide and homicide—they are rather to be seen as ways into the general cultural system. They are folk explanations which are 'the popular means of stating moral and evaluational ideas about

47

suicide, homicide and about "life" in general'. We are thus led towards an even larger unit of analysis—to the culture pattern of the society.

> Since social relationships, social acts and culture do not take place *in vacuo*, we are endeavouring to find the concentration of social relationships and the accompanying idiom of culture which are associated with homicide and with suicide in different human groups. It is 'culture patterns' in this sense that we are investigating. We are interested in whether or not killings, either of the self or of another, form many or few patterns, how the patterns compare, and whether they vary significantly from one society to another.[44]

The movement is, in other words, from the meaning of the individual act out into the social relationships which are associated with it. In this way one finds out how the society works for its members in a subjective, phenomenal sense.

In Bohannan's other works the elaboration of cultural pattern within a society is continued until one can be said to have access to the 'folk system' of a society. One knows one has reached this point by one's ability to interact with the people in that society. This relates back to our earlier reference to 'being able to speak the same language' as a requirement for getting at the meaning of deviant behaviour.

> The folk system is the ethnographer's action-oriented reading of the concrete, which is sufficiently 'collective' as to allow him to interact successfully with the other people who utilize this system of symbols and culture traits.[45]

This is an improvement upon the ethnographical studies of deviance to which we referred before in that description of the folk system includes not only the deviance but also the social control. However, like such studies, it appears to be culturally specific—to be elevating the folk system into a unique—and thus by definition incomparable—phenomenon.

This is indeed how the approach via the folk system has been interpreted. The irritation felt by sociologists who find themselves unable to use the findings of ethnographic studies within their general theories, was paralleled by the irritation of anthropologists

48

who felt themselves to be warned off using Bohannan's material on the Tiv, by virtue of his insistence upon the necessity of understanding every element as part of the total system. Gluckman complained that 'the insistence on the cultural vagueness of folk systems seems to [him] continually to distract Bohannan's attention from those *similarities within differences* that enable one to formulate more clearly both the problem of a simple society's law and those of comparative law'.[46]

The ethnographic approach which is under attack here does not however make comparative analysis difficult because of its stress upon the 'vagueness' of folk systems. What is being said is that any society must be first seen *in its own terms* before any comparative work should start. We must not get comparative too early in our work for if we do we will be forced to be reliant upon theoretical schemes, upon systems of meaning, which we have brought with us from other cultures. There is no reason why one should not eventually compare provided one has a way of preserving the integrity of the elements under comparison.

Is this showing an over-sensitivity to the data? There are certainly those who are impressed enough by the similarities between forms of deviance and social control in different societies to want to set to work with general schemes of categorization. We have encountered this tendency in our discussion of the evolutionary comparative analysts. The possession of an overall theory of the development of social control militates against the idea of spending time assembling a variety of complete folk systems for comparison.

We can summarize the problems we have been discussing in two ways. We will firstly use a 'genealogy of comparative methods' borrowed from Bohannan to locate the studies to which we have referred.[47] In this a distinction is initially made between 'casual' and 'controlled' comparison and these are then sub-divided:

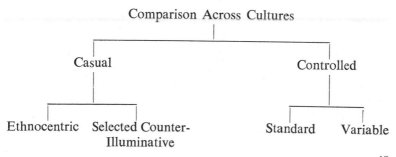

Comparison Across Cultures

Casual   Controlled

Ethnocentric   Selected Counter-   Standard   Variable
               Illuminative

Casual comparison is used by the writer to help his reader adjust 'the ethnography at hand to the vicissitudes either of the reader's own culture or some other culture he already knows'. In its *ethnocentric* mode it takes examples from the culture of the writer and the reader. In our survey this type of practice is best exemplified by those writers who engage in conceptual diffusion, who import concepts like subculture and social disorganization in order to make the reader feel at home amongst deviant forms in an alien culture. The second mode of casual comparison refers to the provision of selected counter-illuminative information. This type of comparative procedure involves the selection of instances from other authors to illuminate the case at hand. An almost classic example of this is provided by Bloch and Niederhoffer's *The Gang: A Study in Adolescent Behaviour.*[48] The authors' argument is that under the right conditions adolescent gangs arise in both primitive and modern societies. Gangs provide 'the same psychological content and function as the more formalized rituals (puberty rites) found in other societies'.[49] The evidence for this depends not upon the detailed analysis of any primitive society but rather upon the selection of certain features from existing studies of puberty rites (decoration, tattooing, special language) and the juxtaposition of these with certain other cultural features of adolescence in contemporary American society.

Bohannan's other type of cross-cultural comparison—*controlled*—refers to a more complex form of analysis. Firstly he distinguishes controlled *comparison with a standard*. This involves the selection of some theory or standard against which one's ethnographic material is placed. At times this theory or standard will appear to be of great help in comprehending the material, although Bohannan feels that eventually it 'bogs down' the research. 'Ultimately one can say only that something is or is not like something else—that helps, but it is limited.'[50] In our discussion we have encountered this use of a standard most clearly in the work of the evolutionists where a macro-theory brings some apparent coherence to different forms of social control whilst leading to a neglect of distinctive forms of deviant behaviour. The second form of controlled comparison described by Bohannan relies not upon the possession of a standard but rather upon access to a set of variables. This type of approach is most evident in the statistical studies to which we have referred, where such variables as larceny or murder
50

are related to changes in prices of wheat or to different stages of economic development. At a more complex level, we may cite the use by Schwartz and Miller of variables derived from the Human Area Relations Files in their study of legal evolution.[51]

The casual type of comparison—whether ethnocentric or counter-illuminative—clearly stands condemned as a way of conducting comparative analysis. Comparative examples are used like counters to be placed here or there according to the predilections of the author. The sociological concept or the anthropological example are called into service extracted from the context upon which their meaning depends. There are also dangers in controlled comparison in that the standard which is used may well impose a pattern prematurely upon the data in such a way as to influence later selection and thus detract from the idiosyncrasy of the system under examination. The use of variables prevents such straitjacketing but raises a problem of correspondence between items more forcefully in that the entire enterprise depends upon the assumption of equivalence between such socially generated categories as larceny, murder, crime and law.

In the preparation of our own approach we must guard against the defects of casual comparison as well as against the insensitivities to data which accrue from the use of certain forms of controlled comparison. But in addition—and this is our second way of summarizing this survey of existing approaches—we must make certain that our approach comprehends some of those elements which we have remarked upon as lacking in other studies. This requires that we extract from this summary of approaches to deviance and social control a range of requirements for any satisfactory comparative study. Such a study should:

(a) Do justice to the nature of the deviant act. This means not simply describing its features, or counting its appearances but also locating it within a system of meaning.

(b) Do justice to the nature of social control. This involves not simply a description of the variety of means of social control in society and their inter-relationship but also an account of the enforcing processes themselves.

(c) Do justice to the character of the relationship between deviance and social control. This involves an examination of the ways in which deviance and control are antithetical, complementary or interpenetrative in terms of their personnel, their structure and their culture.

51

(C)   A COMPARATIVE APPROACH BASED UPON DEVIANCE-CONTROL RELATIONSHIPS

We now proceed to discuss the possibilities of an approach to the study of deviance and control which, we hope, overcomes some of the problems we have encountered in our survey and which conforms to the present requirements of comparative analysis as they emerged from our earlier general discussion. Our emphasis in this is upon the *relationships* between controllers and controlled, between those who sanction and those who deviate. It is this aspect which has rarely been tackled comparatively. Most of the contributions and styles we have surveyed have concentrated *either* upon actual deviance or crime—juvenile delinquency, murder, theft and so on—*or* upon forms of penal system, styles of socio-legal control and so on. A concentration upon relationships, such as we advocate, promises not only a break with the 'social control' unilateralism which we have noted in evolutionary studies but also with the 'deviant behaviour' unilateralism which characterizes those studies of the 'crime-in-different-countries' type.

We suggest initially that 'deviants' in pre-industrial societies differ markedly from deviants in modern societies by virtue of their small degree of self-consciousness and by their lack of 'distance' from agents and agencies of social control.

Both of these ideas are closely related to well-established conceptions of social relationships and individual identity in primitive societies. Basically this anthropological agreement pivots on the *ego-centredness* of primitive man. The individual's fortune is bound closely to all others—indeed it is bound closely to the whole cosmos:

This world view is man-centred in the sense that explanations of events are couched in notions of good and bad fortune, which are implicitly subjective notions, ego-centred in reference. In such

52

a universe the elemental forces are seen as linked so closely to individual human beings that we can hardly speak of an external, physical environment. Each individual carries within himself such close links with the universe that he is like the centre of a magnetic field of force. Events can be explained in terms of his being what he is and doing what he has done. [1]

Ego-centredness is closely related to other central features of primitive societies. Culturally and socially-structurally they are undifferentiated—one cosmic view prevails. These features entail the great likelihood that deviant acts, and disputes between individuals, will disrupt the sociocultural fabric, in contrast to the isolability of such phenomena in the impersonal, large-scale society. Sally Moore emphasizes that

> in part, this is inherently so because of the small numbers, but it is the more so because of the way in which structurally determined partisan commitments spread the effects of what start as individual disputes. The ways in which that partisanship is determined and the way in which confrontations of partisan collectivities are conducted or prevented constitute a basic aspect of public law in pre-industrial societies. [2]

In modern Western societies we find in contrast to ego-centred subjectivity a typical conception of the individual as being autonomous and reflective; the latter requiring the principle of objectivity to be central, in that reflection on self requires the capacity to utilize the standpoint of 'the Other'. Of course, the contrast between the two kinds of society and concomitant conceptions of the individual yields crucial differences in notions of responsibility for deviant acts. The ego-centred form tends to carry with it notions of complete responsibility for deviant acts and relatively little significance is attached to intentions or motives. In contrast the autonomous-man idea correlates with conceptions of circumstantial constraints and the strong tendency to inspect intentions and motives.

In drawing attention to contrasts between primitive and modern societies we certainly do not subscribe to polar opposite conceptions of an evolutionary kind. It is becoming increasingly clear that we have much more in common with primitive societies than was previously supposed in the shadow of evolutionism. In criticizing the evolutionary ideas of Durkheim, Maine and others, Sally Moore with particular reference to private and public legal matters and associated questions of legal liability, argues that

> there are functional analogues of certain aspects of Western civil and criminal, public and private law in all societies because some of the social problems with which these deal are universal. One cannot characterize whole systems by any of these terms.[3]

(Indeed Moore's strictures might well be applied to our own invocation of the ego-centred/autonomous man distinction. There *are* ego-centric tendencies in our society—tendencies particularly among the young which stress the ideas of subjectivity in relation to collective phenomena and indeed to the whole cosmos; viz. the ecological 'movement'. On the other hand modern societies, particularly those of the West, do not exhibit the overall cultural homogeneity which characterized, say, medieval European societies or even more acutely, contemporary primitive societies.)

Moore's ideas concerning functional analogues are extremely important, based as they are on the notion of there being *universal* problems, problems generated by the mere occurrence of norm infraction and attendant reaction to the breaking of norms. What has often been obscured in comparative work on legal systems and procedures for dealing with those who offend norms is precisely the universality of these problems. Rather there has been a concentration upon *surface* dissimilarities, with insufficient probing of underlying, be it all, more abstract similarities. To take another of Moore's examples, 'private' law and 'private' methods of dealing with legal norm infraction are undoubtedly conspicuous features of primitive societies, indeed of many pre-industrial societies, in contrast to the official, 'public' enforcement of a centralized kind that we find more typically in industrial societies. But this contrast between self-help and collective obligation, on the one hand, and official enforcement and individual obligation, on the other hand, can be greatly exaggerated. For example, collective *economic* liability is a prominent feature of Western legal systems as in the cases of insurance companies, business organizations, and so on. But over and beyond the examples provided by Moore we should note such cases as recent trends affecting collective liability of trade unions in industrial strike action. To the criticism that

54

criminal liability is a completely different matter in primitive societies as compared with industrial ones Moore replies that a comparative fallacy is usually committed in such observations, a fallacy of failing to 'compare comparables':

> Retaliatory vengeance killing between groups is not at all equivalent to criminal penalty. What is equivalent to criminal penalty is the kind of individual assessment of character inside corporate groups which can lead ultimately to expulsion or execution. This exists as much on an individual basis in pre-industrial society as in any complex one.[4]

Cases of this kind are invoked here primarily to indicate the nature of the problems to be faced by those who may wish to establish, as we do, a general framework for comparison based on substantive considerations—that is, upon known empirical attributes of different types of society. Clearly our framework has to rest on very general dimensions of variation, dimensions which, in spite of the difficulties of talking in terms having affinity with the evolutionary notions justly criticized by Moore, may overall constitute a mode of discriminating between primitive societies and industrial societies. Our two base-line factors, those of self-consciousness and distance, can be regarded in combination as making-up a *gap*, one which is relatively small in primitive societies and relatively large in industrial societies. In the remainder of the essay we are concerned to itemize and elaborate universal variable features of all societies with a view to comprehending the social and cultural factors which tend to constrain the size of the gap between controllers and those who are controlled. In this exposition we wish it to be clearly understood that in using the terms controller and those-who-are-controlled we do not have in mind an image of their being two mutually exclusive categories of members of any given society. In industrial societies there are well-defined controlling roles occupied by professional incumbents, in other types of society role clarity and encumbency is much less clear-cut.

(1) *Societal and Situational Variations*

We are concerned, as we have said, with the nature of the relationship between deviance and social control, with the distance between

55

the two elements. The comparative analysis of differences in this distance must take as its units of comparison not just specific deviant acts within one society, but must also attempt to characterize the *differences in relationship* between controllers and deviants in *different* societies. Below we propose a set of dimensions which offset this distance and which influence the way in which the distance will be bridged.

The degree of perceived authoritativeness of the norm: The variation here is between those situations (or societies) in which there is a relatively unambiguous norm that is known by the deviant and to which he accords legitimacy and those in which the norm is perceived as so ambiguous, complex, or partial that the deviant may be said neither to know, understand nor acknowledge its legitimacy.[5]

The smallness, low internal differentiation and tight organization of some primitive societies, coupled with the existence of a generally agreed value system places the average member in a situation where he not only knows the norm well, but where he also acknowledges its legitimacy. He knows the norm and knows it to be automatically applicable. In a larger more differentiated pluralistic society the range of norms will be such that few members could have knowledge of them all. Of those norms which are known, many will not be viewed as absolutes, for they will be seen as representing the interests of particular groups rather than the interests of the whole society; their legitimacy will be undermined by the evident partiality of their initial sponsors (called moral entrepreneurs by Howard Becker) or by their differential contemporary application.

In addition to these overall inter-societal differences, on the degree of perceived authoritativeness of the norm, we may also observe intra-societal distinctions. Despite the complexity, ambiguity, and partiality of norms relating to such matters as driving, drinking, stealing and lying, we find a relatively high recognition of the importance and legitimacy of norms relating to such matters as the sexual interaction between adults and children.

Questions about the nature of social norms and the individual's orientation to them have been a major pre-occupation within social psychology for some time. The principal contemporary stress is upon the ways in which norms shift and change over time, the way in which individuals capitalize upon their ambiguity or decide to ignore them because of their derivation from the activities of interested parties.[6] This emphasis upon the malleability of social norms has unfortunately not received any comparative input, and arguments about the statistic or processual character of social norms tend to be directed more towards discriminating between different sociological theories than towards differentiating the perceived authoritativeness of norms operating in different societies or operative in relation to different behaviour within one society.

The degree of homogeneity of social control: The contrast here is between those situations in which men who seek to apprehend and sanction the deviant can be said to be of 'one mind' and those in which there is a dissensus about the significance of the infraction and therefore about the relative need to pursue, apprehend or sanction the offender. We are used in our society to the large number of groups who are engaged in social control. Social controllers are those who react to normative infractions by invoking some sanction, whether this sanction be described as therapeutic, rehabilitative or punitive. These include not only police forces, secret services, security corps—but also parents, teachers, probation services, welfare departments, the magistracy, the judiciary, and of course the lawmakers themselves. Not only are these groups structurally differentiated in our society, in the sense that they have their own organization, their own role differentiation, but they may also be culturally differentiated by virtue of their respective emphases upon certain aspects of the controlling process. A running debate in our society concerns the lack of cultural homogeneity between agents of social control. The probation service, the police force, the magistracy and the judiciary may all attribute different significance to the deviant act; their common ground is only to be found in the belief that action of some sort must be taken following the infraction. This will not apply in the case of some offences, however, or in the case of other societies. If we continue to operate in terms of contrast then we can speak of those societies or situations in which only one individual or group will be expected to respond to an infraction or those in which the several groups who react to an infraction will be culturally and possibly structurally inter-related to a high degree.

57

It is only in recent years that attention has been paid by sociologists to the complex relationships between different agencies of social control, although discussions of the division of labour in judicial processes in primitive societies have been a common feature of anthropological studies. The lack of homogeneity among contemporary agencies of social control has been well illustrated in studies of the way in which criminal courts work. Matza's sensitive analysis of the working of juvenile courts in the United States illustrates the lack of fit at both structural and cultural levels between different agencies.[7] He describes not only the organizational imperatives of the bureaucracies involved in social control but also the different emphases upon the type of control which should be exercised over the deviant. Similarly Blumberg talks of the way in which one organization in the social control network may exert influences over others in such a way as to influence values and goals. 'Courts, like many other modern large scale organizations possess a monstrous appetite for the co-optation of entire professional groups.'[8] Amongst these groups he includes psychiatrists, social workers and probation officers.

Degree to which an alternative (deviant or criminal) culture is available: The contrast here is between those situations in which the deviant might be said to be operating in a relatively isolated fashion with little organizational or cultural backing from others and those in which he has a distinctive culture to resort to for confirmation of his action, for provisions of resources, for shelter and protection. A predominant emphasis in contemporary American sociology has been upon the nature of the deviant world. The original concern with the gang was primarily structural but the later elaborations of the delinquent subculture were more concerned with the culture of the deviant group, with the sets of beliefs which marked the group off from the wider society. The principal controversy revolved around the solidity of this deviant culture, its relative degree of isolation from the dominant cultural patterns of society. Terms like contraculture and subculture were used to characterize the variations in this relationship. In recent years, the concern with delinquent cultures has broadened to include studies of the sustaining culture which exists for such deviant activities as drug use and homosexuality. These studies have indicated the multiple frames of reference that are available to deviants in con-

58

temporary pluralistic society; frames of reference which are 'solid' enough to constitute *plausibility structures*.[9] In our kind of society there is a wide range of cognitive-evaluative contexts between which we can move and in each of which we can find social support, legitimation and continuous confirmation.

This does not hold however for all types of deviance (e.g. sexual deviance) or for other societies in which the deviant is typically thrown upon his own devices after commission of the infraction. Nadel describes the extreme case where

the loss of social bearings is very nearly complete. Here the transgressor is practically excluded from all normal expectation, left without a niche, and relegated to the role of misfit. In primitive societies it is often unheard of for a man or woman to remain unmarried. Now this phrase unheard of indicates the pressure of the multiple consequences: the bachelor could reach no position of responsibility or authority (whereas in a deviant culture alternative forms of status might become available RR/LT); his economic pursuits would be seriously hampered in a society where the family is the main source of co-operative labour; he might have no one to look after him in sickness or old age, and no one even to bury him or perform the rites of the dead.[10]

Degree to which 'controller's' definitions are accepted by the deviant: The contrast here is between those situations in which the deviant upon apprehension is ready to recognize his deviant status and to acknowledge his guilt, and those in which apprehension and the subsequent processing of the deviant produce no such recognitions or acknowledgement. Again this is an element which has received extended treatment in recent years by American sociologists of the labelling school.

A major interest which has emerged from the work of the labelling theorists is a recognition of the ability of certain deviants to resist definitions handed out by agents of social control. As Fred Davies has remarked in a felicitous sentence 'a recurring issue in social relations is the refusal of those who are viewed as deviant to concur in the verdict'. The classic empirical example of this refusal is probably provided by Albert Reiss' paper on the transaction between young male prostitutes and adult male fellators.[11]

59

Despite the boys' regular involvement in homosexual relations for money, they resist both 'homosexual' and 'prostitute' labels. However, the majority of empirical studies carried out in this area have been less concerned with successful resistance than with the variety of subtle processes by which labels are successfully affixed, by which self-definitions are altered, despite the original resistance of the individual. This is the aspect of labelling theory which has drawn our attention to the significance of labelling in social control itself. In circumstances where the label is accepted without question, then there are defined ways in which the deviant may be treated, defined ways in which he may be allowed to re-enter society after punishment or treatment. When there is resistance to a label, social control is threatened. A deviant who will not accept his status—who will not consider himself 'a queer' or 'schizophrenic' or 'compulsive' or 'an addict'—is thereby keeping himself in 'circulation', he is resisting the type of physical exclusion which is reserved for people who can be persuaded to accept such definitions. Labelling theorists have drawn our attention not just to those who engage in such post-facto resistance to labels but also to the processes by which certain individuals actually decide to embrace a deviant role. It is here that the idea of 'becoming' is of central importance. One considers the possibility of this or that deviant behaviour, bearing in mind the type of definitional reconstructions of the behaviour which are provided by those around one. The relativity of deviant definitions, the inability of social controllers to enforce them, the self-conscious decision to 'become' deviant—all of these are, of course, restricted to particular areas of behaviour in particular types of society. For example, situational sequences which Matza has adumbrated in his discussion of the processes of becoming deviant can only apply straightforwardly to particular kinds of sociocultural setting.[12] Take but one aspect of Matza's presentation, that of *conversion*. Conversion—constituting a switch from one frame of reference to another—is not easily applicable to primitive societies. It might be said against this that members of so-called primitive societies have been converted in large numbers to different forms of Christianity. But our reply would be that what is involved in such cases is a *two-fold* conversionary process. Primitives when converted to Christianity have to be 'converted' to the idea of being converted.

The opportunities for negotiation of deviant identity are similarly

60

limited in different societies and situations. One of us has shown that sexual offenders in contemporary British society are forced to regard their behaviour as the product of determinate factors—psychic drives, sudden urges, blackouts—if they wish to enjoy any type of dialogue with other members of society.[13] Notions of 'becoming' are inappropriate in such a context, where determination of behaviour is such a generally accepted perspective. In primitive societies, the notion of negotiating identities would similarly have much less relevance. For although there may be procedures for determining guilt, there is less likelihood of the deviant resisting the attribution once it has been made; the greater emphasis upon 'strict liability' which has been noted in such societies leaves less room for negotiation of one's degree of responsibility, whilst the limited role structure provides little opportunity to escape the deviant status. Like the contemporary sex offender, the deviant in primitive society may only be offered one self-definition after his guilt has been established.

(2) *Crime and Deviance Distinguished*

At this point we should comment upon the distinction between *crime* and *deviance*. Although we defined these terms at an early stage we have tended to use them interchangeably throughout much of this discussion. This has in a way been forced upon us, in that there are societies, and situations within societies, in which it makes little sense to distinguish crime and deviance. On some occasions the distinction is marginal and on others the two terms have distinctive, unshared behavioural referents. We can choose to leave crime and deviance as undifferentiated in those societies and situations in which there is a high 'degree of perceived authoritativeness of the norm'. In such circumstances the values are common to controllers and controlled. Infractions violate general norms and not just those of a subgroup. It is however important to distinguish crime and deviance in those societies and situations in which the criminal law is regarded with a lower degree of authoritativeness, in which there are a variety of subcultures or subgroups with their own normative patterns, departure from which brings forth sanctions from other members of the community. Our concern with using the characteristics of the relationship between controller and controlled as a way of engaging in comparative analysis is intended to apply to both deviance and crime. For example, within our own society, the four dimensions defined earlier may be invoked to measure the deviance-social control relationship which obtains in the area of mental health as well as the crime-social control relationship which obtains in many areas of sexual deviance. Considerations of the perceived authoritativeness of the norm, the degree of homogeneity of social control, the extent to which an alternative culture is available, the degree to which labels will be accepted, are as applicable to the study of the crime-social control relationship as they are to the deviance-social control relationship.

(3) *The Management of Relationships*

The above discussion of the major factors affecting deviance-control relationships leads directly to a consideration of the ways in which different kinds of societal and situational circumstances are 'managed'. To speak of the management of different controller-controllee circumstances is not to assume, however, that situational problems raised therein are solved to anybody's satisfaction.

The large gap between the upholders of norm conformity and those who deviate from norms in many industrial societies, yields complex patterns of management, not merely in obvious 'big' cases like that of organized crime but in many less dramatized areas. These patterns of management constitute ways in which gaps are bridged. This does not mean that gaps are always bridged for there are numerous examples in industrial societies of controllers giving up the attempt to keep in contact with actual or potential areas of deviance. Such relinquishments would seem to result directly from shifts along one or more of our four dimensions. For example, changes in laws relating to homosexuality—that is, the liberalization of laws concerning homosexual behaviour—have probably resulted from almost concomitant shift in all four respects: decline in authoritativeness; proliferation of differing control responses; diversification of deviant cultures and attendant growth in internal cohesiveness; and decline in willingness to accept definitions of controllers.

62

In many cases, however, the situation is complicated through the generation of processes which are almost entirely *specific to and attendant upon the concrete relationships obtaining between controllers and controllees*. This phenomenon is directly addressed in the deviance amplifying model produced by Wilkins, a model which is concerned with changes in relationships between controllers and controllees over time.[14] In the first place the model allows for a relationship of tolerance, one in which there is knowledge on both sides of norms and norm infraction. This constitutes a state of relatively stable peace. The relationship is typically disturbed by the mobilization of law enforcers by other control agencies who have developed objections to the *modus vivendi*. The individuals and groups who are the targets of the mobilization respond in terms of new methods of defence, accentuation of deviant indentities, and increase in deviant behaviour. More forceful action is then taken by the controllers and more actions may come to be defined as deviant. It is clear that a point will be reached where the controllers' resources are inadequate to eliminate or terminate the behaviour and a truce has to be established (more often tacitly than openly). The initial state of tolerance is now replaced by an *unstable* peace. In this situation the deviant group may have to accommodate itself to intermittent harassment, with the occasional selection of scapegoats as indications to the general community that the battle is being won by the controllers.

This brief sketch of the deviance amplifying model provides some limited ideas as to the nature of controller-controllee relationships in a situation which is relatively autonomous. A relatively autonomous controller-controllee relationship is one which, in comparison with other circumstances, is free of variable factors other than those which have to do with strategic relationships between the two sets. In such circumstances the concern of both sides, and all other parties, is simply 'who can win the game?' The empirically unimaginable, 'pure' strategic relationship is that where: first, authoritativeness of socio-legal norms has declined to zero; second, control agencies have been so differentiated that they themselves *cannot* operate in any cohesive manner and, indeed, their own relationships *vis-à-vis* each other are characterized by uncertainty and lateral bargaining; third, there is a highly pluralistic sociocultural situation such that there are no stable overarching points of reference, where there is a vast number of social vacua available for occupation—

sites where deviance can be mounted—as well as the already existing deviant slots, and the culture is so fragmented that appeals to
higher principles are doomed to failure; fourth, controllees *automatically* resist controller's definitions, constituting a situation in
which all controlling attempts at socialization are *always* seen as
what Loflands calls 'an inverse education for deviant acts'.[15]

This purely imaginary situation was certainly not what Wilkins
had in mind in the development of his deviance-amplifying model,
but there are surely enough *proximities* to the realities obtaining in
a number of contemporary societies to enable it to be conven-
iently used as a means of highlighting certain empirical tendencies.

The imaginary situation outlined here conforms to the popular
use of the term 'anarchy'. It is thus interesting to look at the degree
to which modern societies approximate this condition—better, to
consider the respects in which such circumstances are *avoided*. It
is safe to assume that it is in the interests of only a small proportion of the population that such a situation should prevail—
simply because of its uncertainty and unpredictability. Thus it
seems reasonable to suggest that many mediations between controllers and controllees constitute avoidance forms of management—
ways of keeping in touch, of maintaining some kind of strand of
order-deviance continuity. This is certainly not to think in terms of
overt agreements—although such have clearly existed, as in organized crime in the USA. The main point is that many categories of
deviants and controllers develop interests in the maintenance of
predictability on the part of the other side. This is the elemental
basis upon which complex forms of infiltration and espionage have
been established *within* modern societies.[16]

Infiltration leads to complex forms of interpenetration and over-
lap between controllers and controllees. So much so that identities
can become extremely blurred. 'Perfect infiltration' of a deviant
group or organization requires that the infiltrator be a 'good member'. Such tendencies can in the extreme case result in major pro-
portions of time and resources being spent in making *the counter-
group or agency work more effectively*. This can well be a situation
of some significant stability. For it involves the possibility of both
controllers and controlled having a share in the conduct of each
other's affairs. Again, as we have sketched the scene, this is an
extreme case. Nevertheless the situation in which 'the legal order
is both controlling and controlled by the organizations which pro-
64

vide the vices' is hardly unfamiliar to observers of Western societies.[17] This falls short of the kind of symmetrical interpenetration noted above, conforming more to a situation of symbiosis. These forms of symbiosis are most frequently manifested in the relationships between law-enforcement agencies and groups or organizations of professional criminals:

> Given the criteria by which law-enforcement agencies are judged and the conflicting cross-pressures they are subjected to, it is virtually impossible for a law-enforcement system to operate effectively and efficiently without developing policies and practices which are mutually advantageous to professional criminals *and* the legal system.[18]

Interpenetration and symbiosis are not, however, the only modes of managing the gap. These are forms of 'keeping in touch'—ways of bridging a widening gap. Another process of management is that which involves making norm infraction a matter not for controllers *per se* but for settlement amongst what we have here called controllees; in other words norm infraction is made a matter of civil and not criminal law. This injection of a *horizontal* aspect to the gap relationship recalls (in no far-fetched manner) the salience of self-help, feuding practices in primitive societies. This is not to say that we are likely in the near future in Western societies to regard, say, homicide 'as a "civil" offence, so that even murderers can, after payment of . . . compensations resume their normal place in the community'—a norm which is quite widespread in primitive societies.[19] But there are realistically envisageable modes of control which involve controllees becoming their own controllers. The managing process that involves widening the control obligations of controllees and diminishing those of controllers is clearly a significant feature of modern societies and, we might add, a sociological corollary of much recent discussion about the difficulties of monitoring and policing behaviour patterns. Obviously many industrial societies have already taken steps in this direction. An adjacent development—if we can yet call it that—concerns the idea of attenuating the strong emphasis upon *individual* legal liability in Western societies. We have already noted the extent to which in such societies individuals are increasingly backed-up by collectivities such as insurance companies, trade unions, and so on. But

65

the, heretofore only legislative, attempts which have been made to 'collectivize' organized crime—to make it a criminal offence to belong to illicitly oriented collectivities—are, we would contend, also symptomatic of a blurring of well-demarcated controller/controllee distinctions.[20] It is indeed the contrast between the highly centralized nature of modern societies (the very fact of centralization being intimately bound-up with notions of collective identity) on the one hand, and the socio-legal conception of ultra-individualism on the other, which in one respect sums up the controller-controllee gap. Distance is so large in modern societies because the gap exists to all intents and purposes between a highly centralized political system and a single individual, the society as a collectivity processing the responsible individual.

(4) *Conclusion*

We have not regarded the statement of prescriptions as part of our task. As we said at the outset our major aim is to assist in the clarification of law-and-order phenomena through the adoption of a comparative perspective. It would, however, be foolish to deny that our discussion has no prescriptive relevance—if only for the simple reason that the propagation of a wider or a more general viewpoint in itself relativizes the normal perceptions of a particular problem. Relativization does not in this respect entail anything more than 'putting things in perspective'. Providing a perspective—in our case one which emerges from focussing upon a large number of different societies and in particular considering salient features of primitive societies—means showing links between social and cultural phenomena which have not often been bracketed together, except by a few anthropologists. This linking process has been attempted in full recognition of what we earlier called the Scylla-Charibdis problem of comparative analysis—the need to move as sensitively as possible between that which is thought to be true of all or most societies and that which is true of only one, or even a small segment of a single, society. Even though we have been careful to avoid the entirely universalistic tack the fact remains that one can only do genuine comparative work in some kind of universalizing mode. That universalizing mode has taken the
66

form in the present essay of talking in terms of variations upon universal themes, themes established in order that we could address as effectively as possible our central substantive topic of relationships between forces of socio-legal control and forces of crime and deviance. To say, however, that all societies have universal problems, even though at the same time emphasizing variations in their intensity, is to introduce the idea that some features of societies which have come to be regarded as demanding eradication may well not be at all eradicable. On the other hand, the kind of universal problems of which we have spoken at some length draw attention to aspects of societies which rarely get such attention in conventional 'law and order' discussions. In these respects, then, what we have said does have prescriptive implications that must await subsequent elaboration.

Finally it should be remarked that although we have been substantively and intrinsically concerned with the law-and-order problem as it has emerged through discussion of works in the area of the sociology of deviance, criminology and to some extent the sociology and anthropology of law, our analysis has a much wider ramification for the sociological enterprise as a whole: Talcott Parsons' well-known statement that 'the dimension of conformity-deviance [is] inherent in and central to the whole conception of social action and hence of social systems' points up the general significance of the law-and-order problem.[21] There has been a strong tendency within sociology during the past few decades to treat that dimension of conformity-deviance as a primarily theoretical, indeed a philosophical problem. We hope that the present essay shows how much work needs to be done in *empirical* terms. Our analyses have been largely addressed to conceptual and methodological problems which bear directly on the possibilities of wide-ranging empirical work. Thus for us Parsons' proposition becomes an invitation to explore the respects in which the relationships between deviants, on the one hand, and socializing and law-enforcing agencies, on the other hand, vary empirically from setting to setting.

NOTES AND REFERENCES

Section A

1. President's Commission on Law Enforcement and Administration of Justice, *The Challenge of Crime in a Free Society*, Washington D.C., U.S. Government Printing Office (1967).
2. Lyndon B. Johnson, Message to Congress, March 9, 1966.
3. Richard Quinney, *The Social Reality of Crime*, Boston, Mass., Little, Brown and Company (1970), p. 310.
4. For example, Jerome H. Skolnick, *Justice Without Trial: Law Enforcement in Democratic Society*, New York, John Wiley (1966); and William J. Chambliss (ed.), *Crime and the Legal Process*, New York, McGraw Hill (1969).
5. See Robert A. Nisbet, *Social Change and History*, New York, Oxford University Press (1969), chs. 6–8.
6. Emile Durkheim, *The Rules of the Sociological Method* (trans. Sarah A. Solovay and John H. Mueller), Glencoe, Ill, Free Press (1938), esp. pp. 47–75.
7. Cf. Kai T. Erikson, *Wayward Puritans*, New York, John Wiley (1966).
8. Adam Przeworski and Henry Teune, *The Logic of Comparative Social Inquiry*, New York, John Wiley (1970). See also R. Beckhofer, *A Behavioural Approach to Historical Analysis*, New York, Free Press (1969), especially chs. 5–7.
9. See Bryan R. Wilson (ed.), *Rationality*, Oxford, Blackwell (1970).
10. Przeworski and Teune, *op. cit.*
11. *Ibid.*, p. 104.
12. Sheldon Glueck 'Comparative Criminology', quoted in Hermann Mannheim, *Comparative Criminology*, London, Routledge and Kegan Paul (1965), p. xi.
13. Przeworski and Teune, *op. cit.*, p. 97.
14. *Ibid.*, p. 30.
15. Reinhard Bendix, 'Concepts and Generalisations in Comparative Sociological Studies', *American Sociological Review*, 28 (1963), p. 532.
16. Angus Campbell, 'Recent Developments in Survey Studies of Potential Behaviour', in Austin Ranney (ed.), *Essays on the Behavioural Study of Politics*, Urbana, University of Illinois Press, p. 45 (1962). This is invoked in the insightful essay by Frederick W. Frey, 'Cross-cultural Research in Political Science', in Robert T. Holt and John E. Turner (eds.), *The Methodology of Comparative Research*, New York, Free Press (1970).

17. Frey (*ibid.*), p. 189.
18. It is interesting to note in this connection that Marsh's useful survey of comparative studies makes no reference to crime or deviance. His bibliographical section includes only fleeting reference to comparative law in conjunction with the comparison of political systems. Robert W. Marsh, *Comparative Sociology*, New York, Harcourt, Brace and World (1967).
19. David Matza, *Becoming Deviant*, Englewood Cliffs, Prentice-Hall (1969).
20. *Ibid.*, p. 9.

Section B

1. For extended discussion of these definitional problems see Laurie Taylor *Deviance and Society*, London, Michael Joseph (1971), ch. 2.
2. For an interesting discussion of this 'search' see George Vold, *Theoretical Criminology*, New York, Oxford University Press (1958).
3. Adolphe Quetelet. quoted in Mannheim, *op. cit.*, p. 96.
4. Emile Durkheim, *Suicide* (trans. George Simpson), London, Routledge and Kegan Paul (1952), pp. 146–7.
5. For a good recent example of such a critique see Nigel Walker, *Crimes, Courts and Figures; an Introduction to Criminal Statistics*, Harmondsworth, Penguin (1971).
6. Donald R. Cressey, *Other People's Money: A Study in the Social Psychology of Embezzlement*, Glencoe, Free Press (1953).
7. 'For in their actual use, categories of crime ... are ... the shorthand reference terms for that knowledge of the social structure and its criminal events upon which the task of practically organizing the work of 'representation' is premised. That knowledge includes, embodied within what burglary, petty theft, narcotics violations, child molestation and the rest *actually stand for*, knowledge of modes of criminal activity, ecological characteristics of the community, patterns of daily slum life, psychological and social biographies of offenders, criminal histories and futures; in sum, practically tested criminological wisdom.' David Sudnow, 'Normal Crimes: Sociological Features of the Penal Code in a Public Defender Office', in Chambliss (ed.), *op. cit.*, ch. 14.
8. Aaron Cicourel, *The Social Organization of Juvenile Justice*, New York, John Wiley (1968).
9. Cf. Michael Banton, *The Policeman in the Community*, London, Tavistock (1964).
10. Cicourel, *op. cit.*, p. 91.
11. *Ibid.*
12. T. C. N. Gibbens and R. H. Ahrenfeldt (eds.), *Cultural Factors in Delinquency*, London, Tavistock (1966). These comments represent a summary of part of the transactions of the Topeka Conference on Cultural Factors in Delinquency and are, therefore, necessarily somewhat baldly stated.
13. Preben Wolf, 'Crime and Development. An International Comparison

of Crime Rates', *Scandinavian Studies in Criminology*, Oslo, 3 (1971), pp. 107–20. A recent example of an attempt to examine the problems involved in using criminal statistics as social indicators illustrates some of the ways in which issues of equivalence and comparison might be overcome: N. Howard Avison, 'Criminal Statistics as Social Indicators' in A. Schonfield and S. Shaw, *Social Indicators and Social Policy*, London, Heinemann (1972).

14. *Ibid.*, p. 110.

15. Robert K. Merton 'Epilogue' to R. K. Merton and R. A. Nisbet (eds.), *Contemporary Social Problems*, New York, Harcourt Brace (1961), p. 703.

16. Thorsten Sellin and Marvin E. Wolfgang, *The Measurement of Delinquency*, New York, John Wiley (1964).

17. Walker, *op. cit.*, p. 73.

18. Peter McHugh, 'A Common-Sense Conception of Deviance', in Jack D. Douglas (ed.), *Deviance and Respectability*, New York, Basic Books (1970), p. 65.

19. We do not propose here to provide any detailed exposition or critique of these two perspectives. Amongst the more important examples of subcultural theory are: Albert K. Cohen, *Delinquent Boys*, Glencoe, Free Press (1955) and Richard A. Howard and Lloyd E. Ohlin, *Delinquency and Opportunity*, Glencoe, Free Press (1960). For labelling theory see Edwin M. Lemert, *Human Deviance, Social Problems, and Social Control*, Englewood Cliffs, Prentice-Hall (1967) and Howard S. Becker, *Outsiders*, Glencoe, Free Press (1963). A good sympathetic critique of sub-cultural theory is David M. Downes, *The Delinquent Solution*, London, Routledge and Kegan Paul (1966). A harsher critique of some aspects of labelling theory is Robert K. Merton, 'Epilogue' to 1971 edition of Merton and Nisbet, *op. cit.*, pp. 824 ff.

20. Cohen, *op. cit.*

21. There are many examples of this conceptual dependence. In some studies the researcher does little more than apply such concepts as anomie, maternal deprivation, social disorganization, delinquent generation, to another culture and remark upon its fit. Other studies start from this point but many introduce reservations upon the applicability of the concept as a significant element in the study. The following are merely a sample: Karl O. Christiansen 'Delinquent Generations in Denmark', *British Journal of Criminology*, 4 (1964), p. 250. Lois B. Defleur, 'A Cross-Cultural Comparison of Juvenile Offenders and Offences; Cordoba, Argentina and the United States', *Social Problems*, XIV (Spring, 1967), pp. 483–92; Paul Hollander, 'A Converging Social Problem: Juvenile Delinquency in the Soviet Union and the United States', *British Journal of Criminology*, 9 (1966), pp. 49–67; S. Kirson Weinberg, 'Juvenile Delinquency in Ghana: A Comparative Analysis of Delinquents and Non-Delinquents', *American Sociological Review*, 55 (1964), pp. 471–81; Edmund W. Vaz, 'Juvenile Gang Delinquency in Paris', *Social Problems*, X (Summer 1962), pp. 23–31; Preben Wolf, 'Crime and Social Class in Denmark', *British Journal of Criminology*, 3 (1962), pp. 5–17.

22. David Downes, *The Delinquent Solution*, London, Routledge and Kegan Paul (1966). Downes attempts to suggest why it is that certain aspects of the American sub-cultural pattern are not replicated in Great Britain. He at least tentatively raises the question of the limits upon cultural

71

diffusion.

23. See for example Raoul Naroll, 'Some Thoughts on Comparative Method in Cultural Anthropology', in Hubert M. and Ann B. Blalock (eds.), *Methodology in Social Research*, New York, McGraw-Hill (1968), ch. 7. See also Andre J. F. Kobben, 'The Logic of Cross-Cultural Analysis: Why Exceptions?', in Stein Rokkan (ed.), *Comparative Research Across Cultures and Nations*, Paris, Mouton (1968) pp. 17–53.

24. Donald R. Cressey, *Criminal Organization*, London, Heinemann Educational Books (1972).

25. Ruth Shonle Cavan and Jordan T. Cavan, *Delinquency and Crime: Cross-Cultural Perspectives*, New York, J. P. Lippinco & Company (1968). (We are aware that our statement does not take account of earlier cross-cultural works which relied primarily upon statistical material as the basis for comparison, e.g. Durkheim, *Suicide, op. cit.*; W. Bonger, *Economic Conditions and Criminality*, Boston (1916). *The Subculture of Violence* by Marvin E. Wolfgang and Franco Ferracuti, London, Tavistock (1967), is sometimes talked of as a cross-culture text in view of its attention to culture case studies, but in fact these only take up nine pages out of three hundred, and do not involve much more than the juxtaposition of descriptive material.

26. J. S. La Fontaine, *City Politics: A Study of Leopoldville, 1962–3*, Cambridge, Cambridge University Press (1970); J. S. Le Fontaine, 'Two types of Youth Group in Kinshasa (Leopoldville)'. The summary of this work we have given, by its simple statement of extremes, does a disservice to a study which is sensitive enough to admit of ambiguities and complexities. (In Philip Mayer (ed.), *Socialization: the Approach from Social Anthropology*, A.S.A. Monograph 8, London, Tavistock (1968).

27. Aryeh Leissner, *Street Club Work in Tel Aviv and New York*, London, Tavistock (1969).

28. Laud Humphreys, *Tearoom Trade*, London, Gerald Duckworth (1970); Ned Polsky, *Hustlers, Beats and Others*, Harmondsworth, Penguin (1971).

29. Rainwater, in Humphreys, *op. cit.*, p. xiii.

30. *Ibid.*

31. L. T. Hobhouse, *Morals in Evolution*, London, Chapman and Hall (1906), p. 1.

32. Richard D. Schwartz and James C. Miller, 'Legal Evolution and Societal Complexity', *American Journal of Sociology*, 70 (September 1964), 159–169.

33. *Ibid.*, p. 162.

34. Nils Christie, 'Changes in Penal Values', *Scandiavian Studies in Criminology*, 2, London (1968), pp. 161–72.

35. *Ibid.*

36. *Ibid.* Cf. Troy Duster, *The Legislation of Morality*, New York, Free Press (1970).

37. Yehudi Cohen, 'Ends and Means in Political Control: State Organisation and the Punishment of Adultery, Incest and Violation of Celibacy', *American Anthropologist*, 71 (1969), pp. 658–587.

38. Cohen does in fact hold to the position that all cross-cultural hypotheses have evolutionary significance.

39. Marc Ancel, *Social Defence*, London, Routledge and Kegan Paul (1965). The following discussion relies extensively upon Ancel's article: 'The

Collection of European Penal Codes and the Study of Comparative Law', *University of Pennsylvania Law Review*, 106 (January 1958).
40. *Ibid.*
41. *Ibid.*
42. Ancel, *Social Defence, op. cit.* p. 202.
43. Paul Bohannan, *African Homicide and Suicide*, New York, Princeton, University Press (1960).
44. *Ibid.*, ch. 1.
45. Paul Bohannan, 'Ethnography and Comparison in Legal Anthropology' in Laura Nader (ed.), *Law in Culture and Society*, Chicago, Aldine (1969), p. 407.
46. Max Gluckman, *Ideas in Barotse Jurisprudence*, New Haven, Yale University Press (1965), p. 214. The disagreement between Bohannan and Gluckman is admirably summarized and evaluated by Sally Falk Moore, 'Introduction' (to Part Four), Nader, *op. cit.*, pp. 337–48.
47. Bohannan, in Nader, *op. cit.*, pp. 412–14.
48. Herbert A. Bloch and Arthur Niederhoffer, *The Gang: A Study of Adolescent Behaviour*, New York, Philosophical Library (1958).
49. *Ibid.*, p. 17.
50. Bohannan, in Nader, *op. cit.*, p. 413.
51. Schwartz and Miller, *op. cit.*

Section C

1. Mary Douglas, *Purity and Danger*, London, Routledge and Kegan Paul (1966), p. 81.
2. Sally Falk Moore, 'Legal liability and evolutionary interpretation: some aspects of strict liability, self-help and collective responsibility', in Max Gluckmann (ed.), *The Allocation of Responsibility*, Manchester, Manchester University Press (1972), pp. 74–5. More generally see Neil J. Smelser, *Theory of Collective Behaviour*, London, Routledge and Kegan Paul (1962).
3. Moore, *op. cit.*, p. 74.
4. *Ibid.*, p. 94.
5. General problems concerning deviance, legitimacy and authoritativeness are discussed in Talcott Parsons, *The Social System*, London, Tavistock (1951), pp. 291–7.
6. Ralph H. Turner treats aspects of this theme in 'Role-taking, process versus conformity', in Arnold Rose (ed.), *Human Behaviour and Social Processes*, Boston Mass., Houghton Mifflin (1962), pp. 20–40.
7. David Matza, *Delinquency and Drift*, New York, John Wiley (1964).
8. Abraham S. Blumberg, 'The Practice of Law as Confidence Game: Organizational Cooperation of a Profession', in Chambliss (ed.), *op. cit.*, p. 237.
9. Peter L. Berger, *The Sacred Canopy*, New York, Doubleday (1967).
10. S. F. Nadel, 'Social Control and Self-Regulation', *Social Forces*, 31 (March, 1953), p. 269.
11. Albert J. Reiss, Jr., 'The Social Integration of Queers and Peers', in

John H. Gagnon and William Simon (eds.), *Sexual Deviance*, New York, Harper and Row (1967).

12. Matza, *Becoming Deviant, op. cit.*, cf. the sequential approach of John Lofland, *Deviance and Identity*, Englewood Cliffs, Prentice-Hall (1969). See also Robin Horton, 'African Conversion', *Africa*, XLI (April, 1971), pp. 85 108.
13. Laurie Taylor, 'The Significance and Interpretation of Replies to Motivational Questions: The Case of Sex Offenders', *Sociology*, 6 (January, 1972), pp. 23–39.
14. Leslie T. Wilkins, *Social Deviance*, Englewood Cliffs, Prentice-Hall (1964).
15. Lofland, *op. cit.*, p. 83.
16. This discussion of types of relationships has some affinities with the characterization of balances and imbalances in social relationships described in Alvin W. Gouldner, 'The Norm of Reciprocity: A Preliminary Statement', *American Sociological Review*, XXV (1960), pp. 161–79.
17. Chambliss in Chambliss (ed.), *op. cit.*, p. 92.
18. *Ibid.*, p. 89.
19. Nadel, *op. cit.*, p. 271.
20. Cf. Cressey, *Criminal Organization, op. cit.*
21. Talcott Parsons. *The Social System, op. cit.*, p. 249. It should be emphasized that both Durkheim and Weber *did* to a large extent subscribe in their different ways to this kind of view of sociology. Cf. Max Weber, *Max Weber on Law* (trans. M. Rheinstein and Edward Shils), Cambridge, Mass., Harvard University Press (1954).